ENVIRONMENTAL
DEBT

ENVIRONMENTAL
DEBT

THE HIDDEN COSTS OF A
CHANGING GLOBAL ECONOMY

AMY LARKIN

palgrave
macmillan

ENVIRONMENTAL DEBT
Copyright © Amy Larkin, 2013.
All rights reserved.

First published in 2013 by PALGRAVE MACMILLAN® in the United
States—a division of St. Martin's Press LLC, 175 Fifth Avenue, New
York, NY 10010.

Where this book is distributed in the UK, Europe and the rest of the
world, this is by Palgrave Macmillan, a division of Macmillan Publishers
Limited, registered in England, company number 785998, of Houndmills,
Basingstoke, Hampshire RG21 6XS.

Palgrave Macmillan is the global academic imprint of the above
companies and has companies and representatives throughout the world.

Palgrave® and Macmillan® are registered trademarks in the United
States, the United Kingdom, Europe and other countries.

An excerpt of "All Along The Watchtower" appears in the text.
Copyright © 1968 by Dwarf Music; renewed 1996 by Dwarf Music.
Used with permission.

Lyrics from "It Is A Privilege to Pee" from *Urinetown* are used with
permission.

ISBN 978–1–137–27855–5

Library of Congress Cataloging-in-Publication Data

Larkin, Amy.
   Environmental debt : the hidden costs of a changing global economy/
Amy Larkin.
      pages   cm
   ISBN 978–1–137–27855–5
   1. Economic development—Environmental aspects. 2. Economic
policy. 3. Renewable energy sources. 4. Technological innovations—
Environmental aspects. I. Title.
HD75.6.L37   2013
333.7—dc23

2012047885

A catalogue record of the book is available from the British Library.

Design by Letra Libre

First edition: June 2013

10 9 8 7 6 5 4 3 2 1

Printed in the United States of America.

For Max and Rose and Sam and
Maddie and Celeste and Rafa

Researched by Johanna Goetzel

CONTENTS

One touch of nature makes the whole world kin.
—William Shakespeare

*In a dark place we find ourselves, and a
little more knowledge lights our way.*
—Yoda

PREFACE

My worldview connects an inherent love of nature with an abiding respect and admiration for the power and dynamism of business. My parents' values inspired me as a child and continue to inspire me today. Those values are the genesis of this book.

I feel at home in the world of business. My father was an inventor and small businessman (he designed and built machines that made concrete reinforcements for high-rise construction), my mother was Commissioner of Purchasing for New York City, my brother is a small businessman (also in construction parts), and I followed in the family footsteps when I co-founded one of the first affinity marketing businesses. That business, Message!Check Corp., won the City of Seattle Small Business of the Year Award in 1989. I have always believed that robust commerce is a central ingredient to a stable and healthy world—and conversely, that commerce is inseparable from its impact on the world around it.

Starting in 1981, I spent 25 years as a volunteer and two-time board member for Greenpeace. In 2005, just after Hurricane Katrina, I was watching CNN Money. Anchor Lou Dobbs had on three meteorologists from august institutions, and all insisted that climate change was going to increase the frequency of such intense storms. Mr. Dobbs clarified that this would mean that we could expect more events like Hurricane Katrina. And then he said, "I don't want to pay for that." AHA! I'd already been closely watching the insurance industry's participation in the global warming debate. Extreme weather was costing them huge, unanticipated payouts. Indeed, the insurance industry's entire business model was suddenly endangered by the climate's new proclivity toward intense storms and extreme weather of all kinds.

The next day, after Mr. Dobbs connected extreme weather with financial self-interest, I called John Passacantando, then the executive director of Greenpeace USA, and we discussed a new opportunity for the organization. Greenpeace had been working on solutions for years, but now we would focus more keenly on "following the money." There were new equations being born as climate change risks to business were becoming more easily quantifiable. This made the business case when discussing green alternatives.

We first tried to connect the federal flood insurance programs, the reinsurance industry and post-Katrina planning with the realities of extreme weather and likely future costs. Alas, the politics surrounding Katrina's rebuild were too internecine, and we abandoned this effort after only three months. But I joined the organization full time soon thereafter to start a new arm, Greenpeace Solutions.

In my six years as director of Greenpeace Solutions, I helped forge multiple public-private initiatives with a host of multinational corporations and academic institutions, and our work on natural refrigerants received the prestigious 2011 Roy Award from Harvard University's Kennedy School of Government for the protection of natural resources. This work was unbelievably gratifying and exciting.

But my assessment of big business normally resides with its sternest critics. I think that corporations generally want it both ways. They want the rights of an individual to influence policy and the right to use unlimited money to influence elections. Most profoundly, executives and boards use the protection of the corporate veil against liability for their decisions that impact the economy, the environment and virtually anything else that affects people's day-to-day lives.

Yet throughout my work life, I have found kindred spirits at many multinationals, and been lucky enough to witness their leadership, courage, and astonishing innovation. There are MANY people at the heart of companies big and small who feel as strongly as I do about protecting nature. They may not chain themselves to coal plants (neither do I), but in their own way, they are equally fierce. I hope this book unleashes the courage and steely will of all those corporate employees, board members and shareholders who hold the keys to the survival of the natural world in their daily decisions and actions. I also hope the book offers a new toolbox for individuals who want to use their everyday lives as engines of environmental protection—including influencing government.

And, as importantly, I hope that informed citizens demand that elected officials no longer separate the public budget outputs for one item (i.e., medical care for childhood asthma) from their environmental inputs (i.e., air pollution). Our public budgets are unbelievably complex, and I hope this book aids in the process of connecting the dots between the pieces of our spending puzzle.

Connecting financial and environmental debt will require a rewiring of the economy.

I presume that business both large and small can provide underlying security for most of the people in the world.

I presume that business must thrive in order to have global stability.

Finally, I presume that unless business respects the laws of nature, it will suffer along with the rest of us.

Each of us can now influence the course of events that will either preserve or destroy the natural world. Wherever you work within business, government or in your life as a private citizen, you are the nucleus for the change needed in the world.

It's time to be audacious and bold.

1

A FRAMEWORK FOR TWENTY-FIRST-CENTURY COMMERCE

I n October 2010, in a dull hotel ballroom in suburban Chicago, a rare combination of individual conviction, corporate fortitude and strange bedfellows moved a group of executives to transform refrigeration in their industry. The leadership of the Consumer Goods Forum (CGF), a group of four hundred of the world's biggest retailers and consumer goods manufacturers, knew that better refrigeration could achieve a 2 percent decrease in the world's greenhouse gas emissions over the next forty years—an amount comparable to annual global air travel.

So there I was, the keynote speaker at the first CGF Sustainable Refrigeration Summit. As then-solutions director of Greenpeace, I challenged the group to eliminate an exceptionally potent greenhouse gas, hydrofluorocarbons (HFCs), from all cooling technologies by 2015. Coca-Cola, Pepsi and Unilever had been working with Greenpeace and the United Nations Environment Programme for many years to achieve this transition. This was the day we asked the entire consumer goods sector to make the same move. We were all noticeably nervous.

Several companies shared their own success stories and assured the group that it was a reachable goal, but others expressed concerns about the costs of transitioning to natural refrigerants. They doubted that a 2015 deadline was attainable. Fortunately, there was also a palpable feeling in the room that we could find a way to do something extraordinary together. And then at 4:00 P.M., nearing the end of the day, the meeting leader asked a vice president from a multinational retailer, "You'll do this, right?" The VP's face lost all color while he imagined what it would take to achieve this audacious goal. But before responding, he looked at his biggest competitor and asked, "You're gonna do this?" She nodded her head, and then the first VP, still looking shocked, answered, "Yes, we'll support this resolution."

That day, the Refrigeration Subcommittee recommended to the full CGF board that the organization resolve to replace old cooling chemicals (HFCs) with natural refrigerants starting in 2015. I figured that board approval would take about six months—this was a radical step, and the board members were the chief executives of fifty of the world's largest corporations.

Nope. Muhtar Kent, the co-chair of the CGF (and CEO of Coca-Cola), wanted to announce the resolution at the United Nations Climate talks in Cancun, exactly one month later.

And he did.

Nothing except for nature can transform the world as swiftly as can business—for better or for worse. Indeed, the two concurrent crises in the news virtually every day are global financial turmoil and escalating environmental uncertainty. All business, all economies, all living and man-made systems depend on nature. Growing an economy that destabilizes nature is just plain foolhardy. That's why, in this book, I offer a comprehensive framework to connect the causes and solutions of these crises—the Nature Means Business (NMB) Framework.

NO NATURE, NO BUSINESS

There is a change in the weather. And not just from climate change. The environmental news has become so consistently terrible that its effects on business are now undeniable, unpredictable and damned expensive. In multinational boardrooms and executive suites across the world, attitudes toward environmental needs and responsibilities are changing as environmental problems start to derail corporate success—even survival.

Such shifts directly conflict with every corporation's strong imperative to cut costs in the short term. If a company invests heavily in dramatic changes that will secure its environmental and fiscal future, it is likely to endure some lousy quarterly earnings. This is because today's rules and regulations encourage businesses to separate long- and short-term choices. Investing in new green technology and systems costs a lot on the front end, and the resulting savings might not materialize for many years. These savings have countless long-term benefits, including protecting a company's current position amid changing regulations, propelling a company into a new market position, securing more predictable costs and revenues and protecting the environment. But at the moment, stock market pressures and job security usually collude firmly on the side of quarterly earnings.

Logically, if today's actions cause grave environmental consequences in the future, then they should *not* be logged as quarterly profits—not now, not ever. In fact, they should be logged instead as *environmental debt*. The term "environmental debt" is defined as polluting and/or damaging actions that will cost other parties (people, businesses or governments) real money in the future. And just like any other debt, at some point the bill will come due.

We often overlook the fact that a toxic natural world threatens personal health as well as corporate health. From the stratosphere where satellites roam, to the kitchen sink where we wash the dishes, money and nature are always interconnected.

Until we connect the profitability of business with the survival of the natural world, we will not be able to balance real profits with real losses. This book is a guide to help recalibrate and reconfigure financial choices in the public, private and individual sectors—in government, business and personal responsibility.

Despite the current mania for cost cutting and deregulation, it is evident that business rules and standards must protect the world that business inhabits. The old rules are failing us miserably in this regard. Companies are learning the hard way that the environmental landscape factors into virtually every financial and commercial transaction. Extreme weather in Pakistan, Ukraine and Brazil spikes the cost and curtails the availability worldwide of cotton, wheat and soy, respectively.[1] And during the summer 2012 drought, Canadian farmers earned more money from their solar installations than from their stunted, dry corn.[2]

NO HEALTHY ECOSYSTEM, NO HEALTHY ECONOMIC SYSTEM

In the twentieth century, most business functioned as if there were no limits on natural resources. Just as many governments accrued financial debt that will fall onto future generations, most big businesses profited at the expense of the environment. This no longer works, not for business, not for society at large and not for you and me. However seductive it is to enjoy the short-term financial benefits and phenomenal convenience and pleasure that come with this huge environmental debt, it is as financially wise as sending a teenager to a mall with a credit card.

In the twenty-first century, governments are already agonizing under the weight of financial debt. This will only get worse as water shortages, extreme weather, and industrial and agricultural toxic spills increase the pressure on public spending.

But there is a way out of this. In fact, as you will see throughout this book, many businesses are working with rivals to improve and align environmental and financial performance. It is time for good policy to incentivize more companies to move in this direction and for consumers to put our money where our mouths are.

> "There must be some way out of here," said the joker to the thief.
>
> "There's too much confusion, I can't get no relief.
>
> Businessmen, they drink my wine, plowmen dig my earth,
>
> None of them along the line know what any of it is worth."
>
> —Bob Dylan, "All Along the Watchtower"

Twentieth-Century Business Rules Use Incomplete Metrics to Measure Performance

1. Pollution is largely free to the polluter.
2. Earnings statements do not include long-term financial, economic and social impacts.
3. Governments subsidize business with no concern for environmental impact.

This model no longer works. Here's what can.

The Nature Means Business (NMB) Framework

1. Pollution can no longer be free and can no longer be subsidized.
2. The long view must guide all decision making and accounting.

3. Government plays a vital role in catalyzing clean technology and growth while preventing environmental destruction.

WHAT'S THE REAL COST OF POLLUTION?

As Erin Brockovich memorably says in the movie that bears her name: "They dream about being able to watch their kids swim in a pool without worrying that they'll have to have a hysterectomy at the age of twenty. Like Rosa Diaz, a client of ours. Or have their spine deteriorate, like Stan Blume, another client of ours. So before you come back here with another lame-ass offer, I want you to think real hard about what your spine is worth, Mr. Walker. Or what you might expect someone to pay you for your uterus, Ms. Sanchez. Then you take out your calculator and you multiply that number by a hundred. Anything less than that is a waste of our time."

1. Pollution Can No Longer Be Free and Can No Longer Be Subsidized

We take for granted that government debt can destabilize economies and that individual debt can be a step on the road to ruin. Yet pollution cripples our economy daily with debt that is hidden in plain sight. A polluter is allowed to shift the environmental cost of its actions to other parties, so goods and services appear cheaper than their true cost. This pollution can be as abstract as where your electricity comes from or as down-to-earth as how you maintain your garden and diet.

In 2011, Harvard's Institute for Global Health and the Environment released a study showing that just in the United States, the unreported life cycle costs of coal are between $350 and $500 billion a year. These hundreds of billions of dollars represent actual

Total Annual Cost Estimates in $Billions (2008 USD), and Cents per kWh Above Current Market Prices for Coal-Fired Electricity (Round Numbers)

	Estimated Costs in 2008 (USD)		
	Low	Best	High
Totals	$175B	$345B	$523B
Added Costs in ¢/kWh	9¢	18¢	27¢

Courtesy New York Academy of Sciences/Harvard Medical School Institute of Global Health and the Environment

bills paid by unwitting families, fisheries, businesses, schools, municipal water systems and health-care providers as well as the victims of asthma, black lung and other medical problems. So, despite conventional wisdom, coal is not a cheap energy. Its price is cheap only because it is subsidized by its own victims.

An equally vexatious problem is much closer to home. Pesticides are everywhere—in our gardens, refrigerators, even our cosmetics. In 2007, the College of Family Physicians of Canada published a peer-reviewed survey of the scientific literature on the relationship between pesticides and cancer. It is sobering reading, especially concerning the dangers to children. Pesticides were linked to increased rates of leukemia, brain cancer and non-Hodgkin's lymphoma. Other cancers are strongly suspected to have links to pesticide exposure as well. The study says: "Increased rates of all types of leukemia were found in children whose parents used insecticides in the garden and on indoor plants and whose mothers had been exposed while pregnant."[3] Statistics are similar for other cancers. The extra cost of organic products does not feel so unreasonable when one considers that pesticide-laden agriculture achieves its large yields and cheap costs by incurring this kind of environmental debt.

Right now, pesticide manufacturers are not paying the health-care costs of those afflicted with medical problems triggered by their products. Other businesses, taxpayers and health-care systems are. Just as with coal, the pesticide industry is subsidized by its own victims.

NO COST FOR POLLUTION, NO REAL SAFETY

> Long-term impact is explained in *Star Trek IV: The Voyage Home:*
>
> MR. SPOCK: To hunt a species to extinction is not logical.
>
> CAPTAIN KIRK: Ironic. When man was killing these creatures he was
>   destroying his own future.

2. The Long View Must Guide All Decision Making and Accounting

The inability of the financial industry to correctly calculate risk is now well documented and broadly understood. The global economic meltdown between 2007 and 2009 was caused by individuals and companies reaching for short-term profits while ignoring long-term value. In 2010, when Wall Street rewarded its workers with $90 billion of *legal* bonuses, people from all walks of life began to question the rules and the definition of "profits."[4] The Wall Street bonus structure rewarded those who delivered short-term profits rather than long-term value. Virtually all of us agree that this reward structure is warped.

But we haven't yet connected environmental actions from the past with the costs and suffering they cause today. Old logging regimes from decades ago in far-off lands can harm us today while washing our hands with advanced chemicals may diminish whole ecosystems decades from now.

Remember the catastrophic 2011 floods in Thailand? They were the result of heavy rains *coupled* with deforestation that occurred throughout the twentieth century. Although the Thai government banned all commercial logging in 1989, the damage was largely already done. Deforestation continued after the ban due to a combination of corrupt officials, agricultural needs and industrial demands. By 2011, the massive deforestation had degraded Thailand's topsoil, and without enough trees, the ground was unable to soak up water at a rate that would have contained the destruction. Local Thai factories that produced car parts were closed for months. These closures caused shortages for Toyota and Honda, and both companies were forced to suspend manufacturing in Kentucky, Singapore and the Philippines.[5] Toyota alone lost production of 260,000 vehicles (3.4 percent of its previous annual output), and tens of thousands of workers lost their jobs.[6] This logging from the twentieth century caused financial havoc around the world in 2011, a good twenty years after much of it occurred.

An example of latent consequences in our kitchens and bathrooms is the explosion of products used for antibacterial cleaning, such as soaps, toothpaste and personal care products. Many of these ubiquitous products contain triclosan, a compound that can cause mild problems, such as skin irritation and allergies, in some people. It can also cause long-term, ecosystem-altering problems, such as endocrine disruption that affects wildlife, humans and the aquatic ecosystem.[7] What's more, these products encourage the buildup of antibiotic resistance, which leads to the evolution of superbugs. This will fundamentally alter modern medicine's very ability to treat infection. Whoa . . . think twice before using hand sanitizer; after all, the U.S. Food and Drug Administration states that regular soap and water (or alcohol) will do the same job.

Leading scientific and medical institutions have published findings in the last decade showing that triclosan exposure at low levels causes thyroid disruption in frogs. Human and frog thyroid signaling systems are nearly identical. Triclosan can cause reproductive problems that harm local fisheries.[8] No safe level has been established, and the questions only get more troubling as these products proliferate.

Triclosan is now banned in household products in Canada, and the European Union is attempting to do the same.[9] Businesses built on strong antibacterial product lines have plenty to worry about.

Globalization is not just a buzzword. No industry is local anymore, and neither is any environmental problem. And as important, no industry's impact is limited to its present-day activities.

Moon landing, 1969.

Courtesy of NASA

3. Government Plays a Vital Role in Catalyzing
Clean Technology and Growth while
Preventing Environmental Destruction

Government built and still maintains the infrastructure for twentieth-century electricity, transportation, communications, water and sanitation. After World War II, the United States even helped Europe rebuild its infrastructure through the Marshall Plan, understanding that a functioning Europe was necessary for U.S. financial growth and security. But today in the United States, there is huge public pressure to eliminate spending for basic infrastructure, even though ours currently receives an overall grade of "D" from the American Society of Civil Engineers.

Safe and efficient infrastructure is imperative for an economy to grow, and governments use current tax dollars or incur debt by floating bonds to pay for it. Upgrading systems that benefit all of society, including business, is a good reason to incur debt. In the 1950s, when the United States built an extensive interstate highway system and developed facilities and technology for air travel, commerce, tourism and trade, all grew exponentially. Twenty-first-century clean energy infrastructure, energy efficiency upgrades and low-intensive agriculture are both the solution to the current employment crisis *and* the best way to lower our environmental debt.

Perhaps the government-funded infrastructure we most take for granted today is Internet technology. It was first developed by the Department of Defense in the 1960s and 1970s and then catapulted to its full potential by the High Performance Computing Act of 1991, sponsored by then-Senator Al Gore.[10] This is where the joke about Al Gore inventing the Internet comes from—he actually deserves tremendous credit for championing this bill, which was the funding cornerstone of the information superhighway.

Before launching Netscape, Marc Andreessen, the coauthor of the first Web browser, said: "If it had been left to private industry,

2009 Report Card for America's Infrastructure

Aviation	D
Bridges	C
Dams	D
Drinking Water	D−
Energy	D+
Hazardous Waste	D
Inland Waterways	D−
Levees	D−
Public Parks and Recreation	C−
Rail	C−
Roads	D−
Schools	D
Solid Waste	C+
Transit	D
Wastewater	D−

AMERICA'S INFRASTRUCTURE G.P.A.	D
ESTIMATED 5 YEAR INVESTMENT NEED	$2.2 TRILLION

NOTES Each category was evaluated on the basis of capacity, condition, funding, future need, operation and maintenance, public safety and resilience

A = Exceptional
B = Good
C = Mediocre
D = Poor
F = Failing

Courtesy of the American Society of Civil Engineers

it wouldn't have happened, at least, not until years later."[11] Today, globally, Internet infrastructure is built with a combination of public and private money. Neither can do it alone.

It is in business's self-interest to support the three principles of the NMB Framework and embed them in every level of operations. Not only is this possible; more companies than you think are actually moving in this direction. Do-gooders, businesspeople and politicians can all agree: If economies are to thrive, business must thrive. But if businesses continue to grow without regard for nature, it is as serious a threat to the financial world as a slew of subprime mortgages wrapped into credit default swaps and sold on margin.

NO NATURAL SYSTEMS, NO CIVIL SOCIETY

Changing the conversation about government and corporate spending policies is one of the first orders of business. Environmental debt must enter the decision-making process as we navigate tumultuous economic times.

Environmental Debt is creating a Web platform for readers to participate in solution building of all kinds. It will allow you to help create the transition agenda to usher in new rules for the twenty-first-century economy, and your role is explained in chapter 8. You, the readers, will write the addendum to this book.

2

ENVIRONMENTAL DEBT

Environmental Debt: The Hidden Danger

Currently, global leaders urge each other and the public to ignore environmental constraints in order to solve immediate economic and employment woes. But according to the world's most elite business association, the World Economic Forum, in 2011 water scarcity was the number two threat to the world's financial health. Financial market instability was number one.[1] In 2013, climate change became number three. The truth is, basic financial strategy is inextricably bound with natural resources. As serious as financial debt can be, environmental debt is potentially even more painful because it is often irreconcilable. This debt can linger for eons, disrupting complex systems of all kinds—financial, social and environmental—that support both life and livelihood.

Guess who spoke out against global climate treaties in June 2012?
Changes to weather patterns that move crop rotation areas around—
we'll adapt to that. It's an engineering problem, and it has engineering
solutions.

—Rex Tillerson, CEO Exxon/Mobil

A scorched-earth policy puts everyone in danger. If a company's extraction, agricultural or manufacturing practices cause water shortages near and far, the company should not make money—even in the short term, and even if it supplies desperately needed jobs. The price of these jobs would be too high if water shortages were assigned their true cost, either today or in the very near future. This is the essence of environmental debt. Unlike bonds that pay for education or infrastructure, which provide direct and indirect value for generations, environmental debt begins losing value the minute it is incurred—except to the polluter, who profits today and is off the hook tomorrow. This is not an easy concept to understand or communicate in the current economic climate. People are understandably reluctant to take a harder look and embrace a more difficult path when environmental problems often do not feel as pressing as immediate financial obligations.

But we have to. When Hurricane Sandy hit the East Coast of the United States, it was a bad storm made horrific because the melting Arctic ice warmed the jet stream waters and thus disturbed its natural patterns. How much damage would this storm have caused if the water was not warmer? Don't know. But we *do* know that warming air and seas inflict an extra intensity and strange directional forces on weather. These extra costs constitute environmental debt caused by a carbon-loaded atmosphere, and this is likely the new normal. Does anyone think we can afford more Hurricane Sandys? In the United States, mainstream business has a dreadful record of dodging responsibility for environmental protection. This activist antiregulatory pattern has produced astonishing amounts of environmental debt, and the rationalization is always the same, in good times or bad: concern for employment and short-term economic fallout.

Here are a few revealing samples of testimony from congressional hearings on pollution legislation:

U.S. Senate Hearing on Federal Water Pollution Act of 1948

I refer to the unpleasant connotation which surrounds the word "pollution." . . . I am told, however, that industrial waste is not a menace to public health. . . . It is sewage which does the harm.

—E. W. Tinker, executive secretary, American
Paper and Pulp Association

U.S. Hearing on Water Quality Act of 1965

The general public wants both blue water in the streams and adequate employment for the community. The older plant may not be able to afford the investment in waste treatment facilities necessary to provide blue water; the only alternative may be to shut the operation down. But the employees of the plant and the community cannot afford to have the plant shut down. They cannot afford to lose the employment furnished by the operation.

—William R. Adams, president, St. Regis Paper Company

Speaking against new regulations for the power sector in 2012

A new study "finds six major Environmental Protection Agency (EPA) regulations will cost manufacturers hundreds of billions of dollars and cause the loss of several million jobs. The study also finds these regulations will produce negative net benefits to society."

—The National Association of Manufacturers

There are hundreds of similar examples, and the U.S. Chamber of Commerce uses exactly the same language today when testifying or advocating against environmental regulations. Yet a study by the Washington, D.C.–based think tank Center for American Progress tracked unemployment levels along with environmental regulations, and it clearly shows that strong environmental regulation does *not* result in a loss of jobs.[2]

Fortunately, alternatives for near-term employment provide both resource protection *and* value. Instead of building new coal-fired power plants, we can retrain coal miners to weatherize homes and buildings to make them energy efficient. Doing this will create tens of thousands of new jobs in small businesses and simultaneously decrease our energy needs by approximately 20 percent. And while workers are climbing around buildings, they can install solar panels on roofs and in windows, eliminating the need for even more centralized coal-fired electricity.

These processes can foster employment today as well as long-term security on all fronts. Solar installation costs are historically high—an often-used argument against it—but in the last few years, these costs have dropped by half, and new financial mechanisms have been introduced to ensure that many building owners pay nothing up front for solar installation and efficiency rehab. If government policies improve so that all building owners have these kinds of financing and incentive options, the solar industry will boom even faster. (More on this in chapter 5.)

Already there are more people working in both the U.S. wind and solar industries than in coal mining.[3] Clean energy will

> I know there is pain when sawmills close and people lose jobs, but we have to make a choice. We need water and we need these forests.
>
> —Wangari Maathai, Kenyan activist and
> 2004 Nobel Peace Prize winner

undoubtedly create millions of jobs in the next twenty years. Remember that the computer industry barely existed thirty years ago, and in another thirty, clean energy will be similarly formidable. We cannot know what new technology breakthroughs will bring to the economy or to employment. We can only enable and empower them.

Water Scarcity: The Environmental Debt Past Due

Las Vegas is out of water. The city cut its water use by 20 percent between 2001 and 2008 by paying homeowners to replace lawns with gravel and restricting golf course water use. But the crisis persists. After all, if you're out of water, a 20 percent reduction doesn't fix much. The Southern Nevada Water Authority is now trying to construct a $3.5 billion, 327-mile pipeline to tap aquifers beneath nearby cattle ranches, and it has even suggested refashioning the entire continent's water table by diverting floodwaters from the Mississippi River toward the Rocky Mountains.[4]

When Mickey Cohen and Bugsy Siegel built Las Vegas in the 1950s, they presumed that they could exercise control over the water table with sheer muscle. But even these storied tough guys couldn't erase the environmental debt created by building a major city where there is no water. The recent Las Vegas building boom has bankrupted the city both environmentally and financially. In the not-too-distant future, the consequences of this environmental debt will prove more devastating for the region and its residents and businesses than the severe financial hardship they are facing today.

Southern California isn't faring that much better than Nevada. The Colorado River Aqueduct opened in 1939, and in 1955 it was recognized by the American Society of Civil Engineers as one of the "Seven Wonders of American Engineering." It traverses over 250 miles through mountains and deserts on its journey from

FROM THE OSCAR-WINNING 1974 FILM *CHINATOWN*

NOAH CROSS: Either you bring the water to L.A. or you bring L.A.
to the water.

the river to Southern California. Despite its engineering marvels, it has spawned wars, bribery, dirty politics and, most significantly, population, agriculture and industrial growth where there is no water.

San Diego is the eighth largest city in the country with an arid climate that receives fewer than twelve inches of rain a year. Yet it is covered with manicured lawns and orchards aplenty. San Diego's Water Agency is now in court, fighting the rest of Southern California's municipalities (and the 19 million people, businesses and farmers they represent) over who can use the region's scarce water resources. This court case is the canary in the coal mine for water fights to come.[5]

As the Southwest struggles with water shortages, the nation's overall economy and agriculture will surely suffer. And no one can predict the long-term effects of such dire water scarcity. Great and mighty civilizations, from the Mesopotamians to the Mayans, have disappeared due to water depletion, and it would be sheer hubris to presume we are above this fate.

On the other side of the world, water scarcity dealt Coca-Cola a serious blow in 2004. Local governments closed its Kerala, India bottling plant because the company used too much water, disrupting the local supply, and area farmers and villagers revolted. Although Coca-Cola adopted a very strong water policy in 2006 and subsequently spent billions of dollars protecting its primary ingredient, its old policies still threaten its reputation in India and other important growth markets. Today the company recognizes that its reign as one of the world's top brands depends on its good name as well its good water policies.

But nothing is simple. There remains strong opposition in many countries to Coke, Pepsi and other soft drink manufacturers for the quality and quantity of the water they use, sell and discharge from their bottling plants. Water scarcity, which is exacerbated by climate change, will be of primary concern to all industries, but especially to the $193 billion global beverage sector. In fact, Coca-Cola's Mexico bottler FEMSA with the Nature Conservancy and other conservation groups are spending tens of millions of dollars to protect watersheds that supply water for its factories as well as the region. Francisco Suarez Hernandez, FEMSA's director of sustainability, told me that "the ecosystem is the magic." This is a decidedly new and welcome view toward natural resources. It benefits both the company and the region where the company operates.

Even if a company doesn't care about water per se, industry analysts have developed an entirely new respect for this precious resource. Erika Karp, global head of sector research for Swiss bank UBS, described this new approach to me:

> For any analyst covering a business that uses a lot of water, the analyst has to ask the following questions: Where does the water come from? Where does it go? Who or what is in competition for the water? What is the state of the water when it enters the company's supply chain? What is the state when it leaves? Is there the possibility that water use will be constrained in this region? Has the company gotten more efficient in using water? How else might they be innovative in their business? If the analyst doesn't ask these types of questions that explicitly affect the company's actual license to operate, the analyst should be fired.

The day analysts routinely ask the questions about all natural resource and energy usage that UBS now demands about water is the day that business standards have aligned with the true risk of environmental debt.

The Fossil Fuel Industry: The Environmental Debt that Is Past Due

No matter what we do or do not do, the twentieth century's industrial paradigm will not continue for much longer. Our environmental problems and scarcities will overshadow almost everything else and require that we produce, consume and dispose of stuff differently.

But a new paradigm will not come easily, and many businesses will fight it with all their might. Certain products will have to modernize or risk obsolescence—like the typewriter, the steam engine, the telegraph or, with much greater difficulty, much of the petroleum-based economy. Despite Mitt Romney and Barack Obama's election-season duel over who would drill for more oil in American territory, oil is simply not sustainable as the central ingredient for transportation fuel and material manufacturing. Its environmental costs run too high. But the transition away from oil is gonna be painful. *Really* painful.

The fossil fuel industry cannot be allowed to reap every last bit of profit from every coal mine, oil field or natural gas well, and nations cannot be allowed to exploit all of their own resources at the risk of the planet's climate stability. This is a bitter pill that no company and no politician want to swallow. Nor is the public keen about accepting this reality-based equation.

We need a transition agenda so that the fossil fuel industry can make its money by supplying cleaner energy and resources in the near term. This behemoth of an industry will not go gently into the night. Either its money will have to come from somewhere else, or governments and market regulators will have to develop backbones of steel and demand true market competition based on true costs and real risks.

James Hansen directs the NASA Goddard Institute for Space Studies and is one of the world's top climate scientists. In May 2012, he wrote an op-ed in the *New York Times* about the Canadian tar sands currently being developed by Shell, Chevron, Petro-Canada and a few other companies: "If Canada proceeds, and we do nothing, it will be game over for the climate. Canada's tar sands, deposits of sand saturated with bitumen, contain twice the amount of carbon dioxide emitted by global oil use in our entire history. . . . Civilization would be at risk."[6]

The American Petroleum Institute, ignoring these scientific warnings, states: "The importance of Canada's oil sands stems from the value of oil to our economy and energy security. Global demand for energy continues to rise, and oil sands have the potential to supply much of what we will need in the U.S., while also creating many new American jobs."[7]

Only by correctly valuating the fossil fuel industry's environmental debt, and embedding those costs in its profit and loss statements, will we move to the energy future we need. The NMB Framework shows the path to these solutions. If pollution is no longer free and businesses are responsible for the long-term consequences of their actions, then renewable options are automatically cost-competitive. And taking the long view will almost always lead to energy sources other than fossil fuel. Once government mobilizes the building of the modern energy grid, renewable energy will be the predominant and preferred energy choice. Building that grid will cost approximately as much as going to war with Iraq.[8]

The fossil fuel industry governs much of the world's foreign policy and is integral to almost all commercial transactions. Its centrality in our economy is stunning. And this industry does not play nice. The fossil fuel industry has led such a widespread and effective disinformation campaign, via front groups and paid scientist flacks, that some people (mostly Americans) do not believe in climate change.

Nevertheless, 97 percent of scientists in the world *do* believe in climate change.[9] Evidence is everywhere, and corporations don't need scientists to tell them that their supply chains are experiencing water scarcity and extreme weather events. There *is*, in fact, a change in the weather. Many corporations are betting with the scientists, but very, very few are betting all-in. The need for cheap energy and materials usually overrides the understanding that environmental costs will come home to roost. And for those corporations that continue to obstruct the move to a clean economy, I hope that rival corporations move to the all-in position and work with civil society as if our mutual survival depended on it. Because it does.

Al Halvorsen, the senior director of environmental sustainability for PepsiCo, explained to me with great pride the state-of-the-art manufacturing facility he helped develop for Frito-Lay (a PepsiCo division) in Arizona. The plant's innovations include near-net-zero energy use and a three-quarters reduction in water usage compared to plants of similar size. Everything possible is recovered, reused and recycled, and efficiency and conservation are the governing principles. Al noted that he is beginning to use some of these advances in PepsiCo factories globally, and the company is constantly looking for opportunities to use best practices. When I asked why all the improvements weren't instituted in all of PepsiCo's factories, Al, a conservative businessman and engineer, replied, "It's expensive to make all of these changes. When water costs or limited supply justify these expenses, PepsiCo will deploy all of these advances everywhere. Same goes for energy." Al's story perfectly illuminates the need for a change in the rules. PepsiCo engineers achieved extraordinary advances that will benefit the company and the world—but it and its competitors all need the NMB Framework in place in order to fully deploy this desperately needed work in a financially secure way. Quite a few big companies are in the same boat.

NO NEW RULES,
ENVIRONMENTAL DEBT SINKS THE ECONOMY

The Quest for True Profits

When the U.S. Chamber of Commerce fought climate legislation in 2009, Catherine Novelli, vice president of Apple, stated in the company's press release, "Apple supports regulating greenhouse gas emissions, and it is frustrating to find the Chamber at odds with us in this effort. . . . We have decided to resign our membership effective immediately."[10] Apple, a few utilities, and dozens of other iconic American corporations either left or publicly excoriated the Chamber for its climate position. Nike left the Board in protest. Industries that face the future head-on understand the need for a radical overhaul of the rules. But to dramatize how radical and complex a structural change is needed, look at the recent exposés of Apple's manufacturing facilities in China that show abusive treatment of workers as well as its negligent use of toxic chemicals and water. This was front-page news that tarnished the Apple image. As a consumer, I am fully complicit—I purchased my extraordinary MacBook Air for a very reasonable price. In early 2012, Apple embarked on an overhaul of its production protocols that will likely raise the price of its products.

Apple is not alone in its production norms. The workforce that makes our electronics includes too many children, often works sixty- to eighty-hour workweeks with no overtime and routinely suffers illness from chemical exposure. As Apple transforms its factories, its computers and phones will become more expensive to produce. I would personally prefer fewer and fairly priced (more expensive) gizmos, well-treated employees and environmental protection built into the cost of every product I buy. I recognize this might not be the majority opinion, but it is the way to true profits.

On the whole, the current regulatory system still perpetuates mispriced and underpriced goods, but make no mistake: The era of cheap goods is over. Changing the rules of an economy is not for the faint of heart. Inflation, social unrest, changed expectations, lifestyle adjustments and food shortages are all potential consequences of the repricing of goods. But if you have a serious conversation with a senior corporate executive, repricing is not heresy but inevitability. At the same time, the companies that currently work in niche markets serving those willing to pay for environmental and social costs (i.e., organics, fair trade, recycled goods) may become more valuable, given their deep roots in the sustainable supply chain. Many of these niche companies have been purchased by big multinationals, so the brands that dominate consumer markets are now privy to quite a bit of in-house intelligence on the greener way forward.

The table below lists well-known organic or socially responsible businesses on the left with their multinational parent on the

Earth's Best	Heinz
Ben & Jerry's	Unilever
Tom's of Maine	Colgate-Palmolive
Body Shop	Nestlé
Burt's Bees	Clorox
Odwalla	Coca-Cola
Naked Juice	PepsiCo
Kashi	Kellogg's
Stonyfield	Danone

right. In quite a few cases, these smaller brands are serving as laboratories for new sourcing, manufacturing and packaging for the company's larger brands.

The branding profiles of these organic labels are all well known and central to their success. Most of the time, these smaller labels do not publicize who owns them, and most of their consumers do not know that they are owned by large multinationals. But in the case of government, where the branding couldn't possibly be worse at the moment, we the people own the brand. And right now, the brand is not serving its citizen owners.

Only Functioning Governments Can Get Us Out of This Mess

Reconciling environmental debt poses life-and-death issues, is dauntingly complex and intertwines business with social and foreign policy. Our environmental debt is so serious that national security teams around the world are preparing for alarming contingencies. Whole divisions of the world's military and intelligence operations are devoted to addressing climate change, resource scarcity and energy security. Simultaneously, the military is investing heavily in renewable energy and nonpetroleum transportation fuels. When you imagine the chaos that would result from water, food or energy shortages, it makes sense.

NO ENVIRONMENTAL SECURITY,
NO NATIONAL SECURITY

> Freedom is never more than one generation away from extinction. We didn't pass it to our children in the bloodstream. It must be fought for, protected, and handed on for them to do the same.
>
> —Ronald Reagan

Royal Navy Rear Admiral Neil Morisetti, the United Kingdom's Climate and Energy Security Envoy to the United States, stated in a 2011 speech to Georgia Tech: "Climate stress multipliers are increasing the threat of armed conflict around the world."[11]

Government often does not function as we wish it would. Many government agencies are riddled with red tape and stagnation. And there is a lot of bad faith and dirty money running through the bloodstream of legislative bodies. But the fact remains that the air in American cities is cleaner because of the Clean Air Act. The same is true for the Clean Water Act. Thank you, U.S. government. And when the world's governments actually listened to the scientists regarding the hole in the ozone layer, the 1987 Montreal Protocol banned the chlorofluorocarbons (CFCs) that caused it, and the protocol was signed by 197 nations. Thank you, United Nations.

Industry vociferously opposed the Clean Air and Water Acts and the Montreal Protocol, using virtually the same language they use to oppose global climate treaties and national or regional greenhouse gas regulations today.

While fighting the Montreal Protocol to eliminate the CFCs that caused the hole in the ozone, the CEO of Pennwalt, the third largest CFC manufacturer in the United States, talked of "economic chaos" if CFC use was phased out. In 1975, DuPont, the largest CFC manufacturer, warned that the costs in the United States alone could exceed $135 billion ($580 billion in 2012 dollars) and that "entire industries could fold." As an extra special note, DuPont claimed that the theory is "a science fiction tale . . . a load of rubbish . . . utter nonsense."[12] At the time, CFCs made up an $8 billion-a-year industry ($35 billion in 2012 dollars), employing 600,000 people.

Outlining its vision for America in 2010, the U.S. Chamber of Commerce said virtually the same thing as DuPont had years earlier. Businesses "see a climate change bill and potential EPA

[Environmental Protection Agency] regulations that could significantly raise energy prices and impose new layers of bureaucracy on their organizations. . . . . We also should produce more American energy on our land and off our shores—including oil, gas, and clean coal—which would improve energy security, create jobs, and keep our economy competitive."[13] In fact, moving all new energy investment into renewables and efficiency would create more jobs, make our economy competitive for the twenty-first century and contribute the greatest value to energy security. It would also help avert catastrophic climate change for our children.

But the energy industry is still in denial. Don Blankenship, the CEO of Massey Energy, the largest producer of Appalachian coal, has called climate legislation a hoax and a Ponzi scheme. "How can they be so confident that man is changing the world's climate?" he asked. In 2009, Blankenship denied that climate change, or "global warming," existed, and he stated: "Why should we trust a report by the United Nations? The United Nations includes countries like Venezuela, North Korea and Iran."[14]

Some Positive Industry Harbingers

Unilever CEO Paul Polman is of a different opinion. According to Polman, "We cannot choose between [economic] growth and sustainability—we must have both."[15]

In addition to leading the consumer goods sector in walking its environmental talk, Unilever has taken two radical steps that are models for all industry. First, the consumer goods giant (brands under its umbrella include Dove, Suave and Breyers Ice Cream) has stopped publishing quarterly reports. This is the first step in separating short-term financial decisions from long-term value. Also, the company has pledged to decrease its environmental impact 50 percent by 2020 while simultaneously doubling sales. The only way it can do this competitively is if industry regulations change—a tall order. But rather than forgo its ambitions, Unilever established a Global Advocacy Office whose purpose is to change the regulatory framework that governs its business practices. Society has good reason to change these rules because so much environmental debt is coming due now—not tomorrow, not in your favorite or least-favorite politician's term, but right now.

A surprising array of well-funded institutions advocates these same rule changes. The Institutional Investor Group on Climate Change and Investor Network for Climate Risk both represent firms with over $10 trillion in assets. They actively support a price on carbon emissions and other climate change regulation. And all of the major financial service companies are part of the International Integrated Reporting Council and the Global Reporting Initiative (GRI). Both groups work to create new accounting standards that incorporate environmental and social risks. Their challenge is to define these risks as quantifiable costs for everyday financial reporting. There are some amazing pioneers in these groups, and among them they have the necessary muscle and money, as well as the knowledge and skills, to transform the basic rules of business. The next revamp of these rules is expected from GRI in May 2013.

In the technology sector, industry giants are racing to achieve the most innovative carbon reduction plans. Starting in July 2012, Microsoft is charging all of its hundred-plus global offices and data centers a fee for carbon in an effort to lower reliance on energy from coal. (Of course, the company is not really changing its primary energy sources, it's buying renewable energy credits so that *other* people can change their energy sources. But it's a start.) In a May 2012 blog, Microsoft CEO Kevin Turner writes: "The goal is to make our business divisions responsible for the cost of offsetting their own carbon emissions. It's the right thing to do." This effort demonstrates Microsoft's serious interest in decreasing its carbon impact. The company's decision comes ahead of global carbon regulations and indicates its premonition that a price on carbon is indeed coming. If public policy facilitated the company's efforts by regulating carbon, there is no doubt that Microsoft would invest in renewables to power its data centers, each of which draws a huge amount of energy. These are billion-dollar investments, but companies can't make the change without government incentives and support. Until then, it's a tough new business environment where only a few dare to tread. Like Google.

Google is investing in carbon reductions more directly. In October 2010, it invested heavily in a $5 billion project, the Atlantic Wind Connection, to build a windpower grid for the mid-Atlantic, stretching from New Jersey to Virginia.[16] This "superhighway for clean energy" would funnel power from offshore wind farms to 1.9 million homes while avoiding the extremely congested mid-Atlantic power grid. And in 2011 alone, Google invested $880 million in renewables, mostly in solar projects. In 2012, the company's renewable portfolio runs over $1 billion.

After a protracted Greenpeace campaign against both Facebook and Apple about their data center energy choices, both companies have launched strong new renewable energy policies. Facebook is working with Greenpeace to develop renewable energy for all of its needs, and Apple recently announced intentions to power all of its new data centers with renewables, starting with centers in Oregon and North Carolina.[17] The fact that the tech industry is accustomed to leading on the innovation front helps them transition to new technologies, as does the fact that its members have the cash to move quickly.

Most of us do not connect our Internet use with energy use. However, the data centers that process our Internet clicks currently use 1.5 percent of the world's energy, and demand is skyrocketing. According to Google, a hundred searches are equal to a 60-watt incandescent light bulb burning for twenty-eight minutes.[18]

How many times a day does the average computer user search for something? Of course these data centers are energy hogs.

Imagine if these high-tech businesses (or new start-ups) had smart government policy and infrastructure investment behind them. Their efforts could help spark the era of clean energy just as they introduced the computer age. That's what government did at the beginning of the tech boom; that's what government can do again. In the 1950s and 1960s, the U.S. government helped spawn the microchip industry through a consortium called Sematech. This early investment in the burgeoning industry was critical to Silicon Valley's success and has obviously paid off many thousandfold. (See more on this in chapter 7.)

The financial research industry is picking up on these currents too. Dow Jones, MSCI and Bloomberg are all increasing their coverage of environmental risk, and every day the *Wall Street Journal* runs a feature called "Weather to Buy or Sell," documenting extreme weather's effect on business. In spiritual life, thousands of churches have groups that address the moral aspects of work life as well as personal responsibility to care for God's creation. And in educational and civic life, every business school boasts a program track in sustainability, while the Occupy movement tapped into populist anger at the current role of business in society. Thousands of community groups work on cleaning up local parks, saving seashores or preserving biodiversity in local waterways.

The Time Is Right Now

Today, it seems, there finally may be enough financial self-interest and environmental awareness that traditionally antagonistic groups are motivated to work in tandem to solve entrenched problems.

Recent history shows we are capable of radical cultural change without completely coming apart. Many of the twentieth century's great achievements would be unthinkable to those born as late as 1950. These cultural shifts enabled the United States to elect a black president and Pakistan, a woman. Gay people are getting married, and "animal rights" is no longer an oxymoron. And a few companies have begun investing in ecosystems as part of business as usual and making investment and infrastructure choices based on environmental impact. But by and large, business rules, regulations and norms remain unchanged.

It is now business's turn for a revolution, to ensure that commerce remains viable for the modern world—and, more important, that commerce, culture and civil society develop a mutually beneficial symbiosis. Some businesses already are tilling these fields. Admiration and respect between many businesses and civil society groups have grown as the two sectors work together on numerous environmental and social campaigns. And more and more, governments are cooperating as well. These collaborations provide inspiration and intelligence, but they are not enough because they function under old rules that make the work harder, more expensive and ultimately nonbinding.

As environmental impacts and civil unrest intensify, more corporations will be amenable to working for transformational change. But these big changes will happen only if individuals within these corporations actively stand up for a new way of conducting business.

There's a lot of talk about changing the rules to improve fairness, environmental security and social responsibility. But at the end of the day, only actions matter. Reconciling these fine ideals with crisis management in public and private finance, global employment and environmental instability is the challenge ahead.

Environmental debt puts food, water and energy security at risk. When this debt comes due, events will likely be even more harrowing than the recent traumatic government and business bankruptcies. Once environmental debt spirals out of control, it is irreconcilable. The NMB Framework is designed to help identify, quantify and then decrease our environmental debt load by reevaluating our valuations.

Lowering environmental debt, which affects every aspect of our lives, must become central in all public, private and individual decisions. Environmental debt must now be added to the list of business basics. It is as important as understanding supply and demand, risk and cash flow.

3

THE QUEST FOR TRUE PROFITS

Accounting for Nature

The history of accounting is as old as civilization, key to important phases of history. Accountants participated in the development of cities, trade, and the concepts of wealth and numbers. Accountants invented writing, participated in the development of money and banking, invented double entry bookkeeping that fueled the Italian Renaissance, saved many Industrial Revolution inventors and entrepreneurs from bankruptcy, and helped develop the confidence in capital markets necessary for western capitalism.

—Gary Giroux, Shelton Professor of
Accounting, Texas A&M University

The more common view of accounting is reflected in this joke:

There once was a business owner who was interviewing people for a division manager position. He decided to select the individual who could answer the question "How much is 2+2?"

The engineer pulled out his slide rule and shuffled it back and forth, and finally announced, "It lies between 3.98 and 4.02."

The mathematician said, "In two hours I can demonstrate it equals 4 with the following short proof."

The trader asked, "Are you buying or selling?"

The accountant looked at the business owner, then got out of his chair, went to see if anyone was listening at the door and pulled the drapes. Then he returned to the business owner, leaned across the desk and said in a low voice, "What would you like it to be?"

A good accountant can save you a lot of agita and a lot of money. And conversely, if your accountant isn't quite above board, you can get in a whole lot of trouble. But what the business world doesn't yet acknowledge is that we are *already* in a whole lot of trouble—because current accounting rules allow incomplete data to pass for comprehensive financial reporting. If corporations were held responsible for the full environmental costs of their goods and services, their entire financial profile would change drastically. Accountants and money managers have a clear choice—to be the seminal leaders Professor Giroux described or to continue using incomplete numbers while knowing better. In fact, everyone who participates in the global economy (that's all of us) has the same choice: Do we continue with business as usual, no matter how dangerous the trajectory, or do we demand a modernized approach for our changed times?

State-of-the-Art Accounting

The good news is that the accountants are stepping up to the plate. In November 2011, Puma became the first multinational corporation to create an integrated report that converted environmental information and data into monetary terms. The company's 2010 Environmental Profit & Loss statement (EP&L) quantifies and monetizes environmental impact and integrates it into the operational P&L.[1] Puma hired accounting powerhouse PricewaterhouseCoopers (PwC) and boutique outfit Trucost, a company whose name sums up its expertise, and together they produced a breakthrough document.

In Puma's EP&L, chief executive officer (CEO) Jochen Zeitz notes: "We believe that the current economic model, which originated in the industrial revolution some 100 years ago, is no longer viable and must give way to a new business paradigm, one that works with nature rather than against it."

The Puma report is imperfect in many ways. It uses assumptions that are in the development stage; it presumes a global cost for water and greenhouse gas emissions not yet established; it assumes as true (but likely cannot verify) the reports of suppliers down the supply chain; and, most crucially, it doesn't measure the environmental cost of goods after we buy them. This is known as cradle-to-gate (we the customer are the gate) analysis. But our usage and disposal often cause huge environmental problems (i.e., landfills overflowing), especially with old electronics that leach heavy metals into ground water and surrounding land. The more comprehensive "cradle-to-grave" analysis, which includes these costs, is the gold standard. (Disposal is considered the grave.) Puma, PwC and Trucost acknowledge all of these problems. But even in its imperfect form, the report is tremendously important, and Puma has showed great courage in sticking its neck out first. And in December 2012, Puma published a "lessons learned" from its first EP&L. The company is already moving forward to create a better accounting mechanism for its environmental impacts.

Cary Krosinsky, former senior vice president of Trucost, explained the process of creating the EP&L over coffee after I guest-lectured at his class at the Earth Institute at Columbia University in New York. First, Trucost burrowed four tiers down through Puma's supply chain to identify who supplies the suppliers. That alone took about nine months. PwC then took the quantified supply chain numbers and incorporated them into Puma's standard operational P&L. The research occurred in three phases. First, the two companies measured greenhouse gas emissions and water usage; then land use, waste and ocean acidification; and, finally, product disposal (that last phase has yet to be incorporated into the report). Many other multinationals are working on full life cycle analyses, and all of the large financial service firms are creating methodologies to accommodate them. In the next five years, this terminology will become commonplace and start showing up in annual reports and shareholder letters.

Puma's courage is already making waves. Its parent company, PPR, owner of Gucci, Stella McCartney, Yves Saint Laurent and a dozen other luxury brands, has promised to produce EP&Ls for the entire company by 2015. And Puma's competitors are now gearing up to do similar reports.

These efforts will be a primary stepping-stone for accountants as they navigate the extraordinarily complex world of twenty-first-century multinational business. Puma opened its operations and books to unprecedented scrutiny, thereby laying the cornerstone for the new business framework.

Key Takeaways from Puma's 2010 EP&L

The total impact of Puma's operations and supply chain came to €145 million per year. These costs came from water use, greenhouse gas emissions, land use, air pollution and waste along the value chain as well as biodiversity loss. The company's 2010 net earnings were €202.2 million; had it been charged the appropriate environmental costs, its earnings would have been reduced by 75 percent.

In the same month, accounting giant KPMG also released a striking report.[2] KPMG International chairman, Michael Andrew, and the special global advisor on climate change and sustainability, Yves DeBoer, introduced the report with this paragraph: "This report shows that population growth, exploitation of natural resources, climate change and other factors are putting the world on a development trajectory that is not sustainable. In other words, if we fail to alter our patterns of production and consumption, things will begin to go badly wrong."

The report then goes on to say,

> The business community needs clear global rules, powerful regulatory incentives, and a level playing field to support it in moving to sustainable growth. . . . *In 2008, the 3,000 largest public companies were estimated to be causing US$2.15 trillion of environmental damage.* . . . Some 60 percent of these negative impacts were concentrated in the electricity, oil and gas, industrial metals and mining, food production and construction and materials sectors.

No matter how you count it, $2.15 trillion is a lot of money.

This is not an environmental nongovernmental organization speaking. This is one of the world's largest financial service and audit firms, an inside player in every sector. KPMG calculated that if corporations actually paid for the services provided them by nature, it would eat 41 cents from every dollar of revenue. For most companies, that's enough to turn profits to losses.

In June 2012, at the United Nations Conference on Sustainable Development (aka Rio+20), the CEOs of thirty-seven banks, investment funds and insurance companies announced a "Natural Capital Declaration," a commitment to begin integrating the cost of natural resources into their products and services. Only two American financial institutions signed the declaration: Calvert Investments and PAX World, both socially responsible boutique firms. But fifty nations and eighty-six corporations (including Walmart and Unilever) took the plunge.

Clearly, accountants are exploring new ways of approaching financial data. Spearheading this declaration, the World Bank called on all countries to put a monetary value on their ecosystems. The Bank contends that these estimates are necessary to ensure that current economic growth does not come at the expense of future growth by destroying natural assets such as water, air and soil.

As these new financial tools are refined, accountants will be leaders in the design and implementation of a more holistic framework for business. Their recent work is already beginning to bear fruit.

Pollution Can No Longer Be Free

In the KPMG report, the recap of climate change damage since 1992 reads like a horror movie script.

- A 36 percent increase in global carbon dioxide emissions
- A 9 percent increase in average carbon dioxide concentration in Earth's atmosphere
- An increase of 0.4 to 0.6 degrees Celsius (.7 to 1.1 Fahrenheit) in mean surface temperature relative to historical means (1951–1990)
- Eighteen of the twenty hottest years on record
- Melting of ice sheets and thawing of permafrost in northern latitudes
- Steady warming of ocean waters by nearly 0.5 degrees Celsius
- Global sea level rise of 2.5 millimeters (.1 inch) per year from thermal expansion
- Growing acidity of the world's oceans threatening marine life
- Rapid diminishment of mountain glaciers in terms of annual mass balance
- Steady decline in the annual minimum extent of Arctic sea ice[3]

The crucial innovation of twenty-first-century accounting systems must be to correctly price the preservation, use and destruction of natural resources. Economist Pavan Sukhdev has been saying it most eloquently for many years: "We must end the economic invisibility of nature."[4] Pollution can no longer be free and can no longer be subsidized. Sooner or later, the biggest polluters will cause grievous damage to the whole *economic* system simply because they will have destroyed the whole *ecosystem*. In fact, the KPMG report suggests that this process has already begun. Currently, corporations do not pay for their pollution even while causing economic harm to other persons, companies, governments and/or places. In economics, this harm is called an externality. And the profit margins of most corporations are not high enough to cover the unincurred costs of their environmental impact. There is huge environmental debt in the system as a whole, most of which is not yet on the books. The current system also rewards the biggest polluter with financial advantage.

For example, acid rain is caused by air pollution carried hundreds or even thousands of miles away from its source by wind. It causes lakes, streams, trees, buildings, animals and plants to deteriorate and suffer. All of these externalities cost *someone* money (i.e., a fishing resort loses customers because there are no more fish or a nonpolluting region is forced to build expensive water filtration systems), while the polluters get to keep their profits—until or unless they get sued. And by then the damage is done.

Encouragingly, there *are* some rules in effect already. In 2004, the European Union began adopting a series of laws commonly known as the Polluter Pays Directives that mandate that those responsible for producing pollution must pay for the damage done to the natural environment, including by the final disposal of the product (the cradle-to-grave approach discussed earlier). Because of these directives, many governments are beginning to demand that electronics and beverage companies arrange for the recycling and disposal of their products. But these laws remain sporadic, sporadically enforced and minor in their current legislative import and impact. As environmental issues intensify, the Polluter Pays principle will likely inform more government and business actions.

The NMB Framework aims to incorporate environmental costs into the cost of goods sold (COGS) of every product and every investment of every corporation. Defining and monetizing COGS—from cradle to grave—is step one in the quest for true profits. These new data can then be used to calculate the real cost of doing business. This will not happen overnight.

Take the Long View

In 2010, Puma redesigned its packaging to save money, materials and water. It eliminated shoeboxes and replaced them with bags made from recycled plastic and cardboard, thereby saving 1 million liters of water and 8,500 tons of paper, plus significant shipping costs. Of course, if this new packaging were adopted industry-wide, shoebox manufacturers, their suppliers and freight operators would suffer a tremendous blow. No one wishes hardship on workers, communities and businesses. But we must accept that some processes and products are not long for this world. Although footwear packaging is not the largest industry, the transition from boxes to bags is exactly the kind of change that must be embraced if business is to move to its next incarnation with minimal pain. And when much larger industries are hit with near-term obsolescence, the ripple effect will be much more shocking. Prolonging the status quo because the change will be difficult is not a viable option. There is no longer any easy way.

Here is a simple example that illuminates the conundrum of mispriced goods and resources. I was in a Greenpeace meeting in 2010 discussing global shortages of a variety of commodities. My colleague Kert Davies noted a most important potential problem. Most Chinese and Indians do not use toilet paper. What will happen to the world's forests if a billion more people start using toilet paper? That kinda stopped the conversation in its tracks.

Seventh Generation, the green consumer brand, provides these statistics on its website.[5]

If every household in the U.S. replaced just one 12-pack of 300-sheet virgin fiber bathroom tissue with our 100% recycled product we could save:

- 1,900,000 trees
- 690 million gallons of water, a year's supply for over 5,400 families of four
- 4.8 million cubic feet of landfill space, equal to over 7,200 full garbage trucks

Common sense mandates that paper from recycled sources be the only kind of paper affordable to manufacture, purchase or sell. Yet currently, the 100 percent recycled paper can run one and a half to two times the price of brands sourced from virgin fiber because there is a real price on the recycled materials, as opposed to no real price for the trees (whether from virgin or managed forests). My friend Kim Duncan, a former banker, has reminded me that "we have always lived in an age of constrained resources, and economics is the study of alternative means to optimize competing objectives against such constraints." Obviously, recycled materials provide a societal benefit by lessening the need for landfills and garbage dumps, lowering current and future public costs for these landfills, dramatically lowering water usage and avoiding catastrophic effects and costs of today's deforestation as it manifests in the future. These properly priced impacts would offset the current costs of the recycling; a comprehensive accounting system would address this perverse pricing signal. Consumers would move to buy recycled paper products because the price would be competitive, if not cheaper.

The Precautionary Principle must guide our actions. It was first adopted by the United Nations General Assembly in 1982 as part of the World Charter for Nature. Basically, the principle demands that before using any substance, material or product, the manufacturer must consider long-term consequences of any product or action. It states: "In order to protect the environment, the precautionary approach shall be widely applied by States according to their capabilities. Where there are threats of serious or irreversible damage, lack of full scientific certainty shall not be used as a reason for postponing cost-effective measures to prevent environmental degradation."[6]

In 2000, the European Union adopted the Precautionary Principle to guide and inform policy, and in 2005, the City of San Francisco mandated that the principle be applied to all its purchases (from cleaning supplies to garbage trucks). More and more court cases from Australia, to Japan, to the United States are alluding to the Precautionary Principle.

Government Has a Vital Role to Play

In the early twentieth century, government tax breaks, infrastructure support and direct subsidies favored the bellwether industries of agriculture and oil. This support enabled and literally empowered the Industrial Revolution, the very foundation of twentieth-century progress, but these subsidies are now way past their expiration dates. In fact, today we risk environmental devastation by these same industries.

In the twenty-first century, regulatory structures must *incentivize* those companies that cause the least financial and environmental harm—those that maximize true profits. For instance, solar power is a burgeoning new industry that will benefit the entire world. Unfortunately, since 2010, there has been a trade war brewing between China and the United States over solar technology. The U.S. Commerce Department is considering tariffs of 30 to 250 percent on imports of Chinese solar cells, contending that China is "dumping" its solar energy products below cost in the U.S. market. China subsidizes its solar industry as if it is a state-run enterprise, providing billions in loan guarantees and price supports on an ongoing basis. These hypersubsidies have the potential to crash the industry even within the perplexing Chinese system. The U.S. government also provided billions in loan guarantees to American solar companies via stimulus funding but stopped in 2012 after some huge blunders as well as organized attacks from the fossil fuel industry. An aside worth noting is that in 2010, the Obama administration also guaranteed an $8.3 billion loan to the giant utility Southern Company for two nuclear reactors in Georgia.[7] This is what government does—guarantees essential energy services that society needs. The only real choice for government is *which* energy industries to support, not *whether* to support the energy industry.

China's low-cost (actually, *below*-cost) exports of solar cells and panels to the United States (and elsewhere) has two impacts. First, it has debilitated or bankrupted many U.S. solar panel manufacturers, which are unable to compete with these unrealistic prices. Second, it benefits ancillary solar equipment manufacturers (those that make everything but the panels) by providing cheaper materials and makes solar much more affordable for end users. For the growing number of companies and financiers working in solar installation, the low cost of panels (due to Chinese price supports) provided the opportunity to grow solar power from a sideshow to a real industry. In fact, the industry grew 109 percent in the United States in 2011.[8]

Without a doubt, China is betting its future on major support to the renewable energy industry. The best resolution for everyone would be if the United States made the same bet—a bet on the future. Government must take a leading role in building the renewable energy industry as a means of protecting the environment while ensuring that the lights stay on.

Yet government is actually proving less reliable than business these days when it comes to environmental protection. In a recent example of the dangerous policy dance between government and business, real estate companies continued to develop large swaths of the southwestern United States, even though no drinkable water source was nearby. In Las Vegas, which has had no water of its own since 2005, governments allotted thousands of cheap building permits, and banks thousands of subprime loans, to developers in the last decade. Clearly neither government nor business demonstrated hindsight or foresight, which made a bad situation worse. The subprime crisis hit this building boom first, with ripple impacts on the global economy. But the water crisis is, in fact, a much more serious problem in the long run. The *Las Vegas Sun* estimates that Lake Mead, the largest reservoir in the United States, could run out of water by 2021. There is no plan in place to address this problem, and the social and economic upheaval it would cause could damage the economic security of the entire United States, perhaps the world. One possibility is that water gets rationed—for lawns, golf courses, showers, toilets, industry, car washing, laundry and so on—and what water there is triples in cost. Another possibility is that millions of people in the Southwest are forced to abandon their homes, industries are uprooted and the region's entire economic base is destroyed. Even the best accountants could not accurately calculate the costs of the Southwest United States running out of water. Yet if building plans and projections were required to include the real cost of water, and the real possibility of no water in the first place, thousands of homeowners and businesses would have refrained from building cheaply in the desert.

Something is rotten in the State of Nevada.

The issue of water—access, cleanliness, shortages—has not gone unnoticed. Many mainstream companies are focusing on water as a new primary driver. Fidelity has an advertising campaign that offers surprising information on the quantity of water needed for producing everything from a burger (635 gallons) to a cup of coffee (35 gallons). The company highlights the planet's dire water situation to demonstrate foresight on where and how to find the next smart investment arena. Clearly the big money is noticing the water problem.[9] And *Fortune* magazine's headline, in its October 2011 issue, asks, "Is Water the Gold of the 21st Century?"[10]

In fact, water shortages and the birth of accounting have a shared history.

A Brief History of Externalities

Accounting as a discipline was born of the Agricultural Revolution in Sumeria around 3,000 B.C. These first food surpluses created a need to measure costs in order to correctly price goods, so traders developed the world's first codified accounting system. Alas, the Sumerians did not account for the impact of their irrigation systems. How could they have known that their amazing new agricultural technologies would lead to the collapse of the Middle East's water basin when the soil became oversalinated and eventually precipitate the downfall of their great civilization? They could not. But today, we *do* know the potential consequences of our actions, and we can account for them appropriately if we choose to do so.

We have to take the lessons from the Sumerians. The unintended effect of irrigation was perhaps the first known example of what economists call an externality.

Another fallen civilization is ancient Venice. At the height of this city-state, a flood of international trade necessitated a more complex accounting system. In the late fifteenth century, the

Venetians brought us double-entry accounting, whereby equity equals assets minus liabilities. Yet Venice, to this day, illustrates the real cost of incomplete accounting.

Visitors to Venice can barely conceive what its settlers were thinking when they built this extraordinary place. The beauty of the waterways, palazzos and lagoons boggle the mind, and certainly the founders never anticipated their creation falling into the sea. In the fifteenth and sixteenth centuries, Venetians built hydraulic projects to prevent the lagoon from turning into a marsh.[11] By doing so, they reversed the natural evolution of the lagoon and launched a slow downward spiral for the area's complex marine ecosystem. Complex systems cannot be jury-rigged without unintended consequences—not in 3000 B.C., not in A.D. 1500 and not today.

In the second half of the twentieth century, northern Italy experienced an economic miracle. After being ravaged in World War II, it embarked on a mission to industrialize its agrarian economy, digging a deepwater Adriatic port so supertankers could dock at Porto Marghera, just outside Venice. While it was a boon to the burgeoning petrochemical industry, the new port damaged the region's entire ecosystem by changing the composition of the seabed throughout the lagoon. In some parts, the water became so silty it was impassable, and many native species died out.

I was lucky enough to live in the Veneto (the region surrounding Venice) in the mid-1990s, when I was the executive producer at Fabrica, Benetton's Institute of Arts and Communication. The region was still on a big upswing and full of the excitement of new wealth. But the consequences of poor planning were already evident just thirty-five years into this boom.

The roads were overrun with traffic. Imagine Italian drivers rushing along old two-lane country roads that now served boom towns and new factories. (I tried not to drive much.) The beaches and waters were dangerously polluted, interrupting the pleasures of world-famous Venetian maritime cuisine as well as swimming in either the Mediterranean or in the Adriatic Sea. Agricultural and chemical runoff routinely leaked into the aquifers, and no one local would ever drink water from the tap.

And today Venice is literally sinking—from the big changes imposed on its complex lagoon systems for centuries, especially in the last fifty years. Around the time of Venice's peak in A.D. 421, the standard sea level of the Adriatic was almost six feet lower than it is today. Italy's economic miracle threatens one of Western civilization's most wondrous sites. This fleeting wealth will be viewed in the rearview mirror with sad and angry eyes.

The Case for Unified Financial Reports That Include Externalities

> There are known knowns; there are things we know we know. We also know there are known unknowns; that is to say we know there are some things we do not know. But there are also unknown unknowns—there are things we do not know we don't know.
> —U.S. Secretary of Defense Donald Rumsfeld, 2002

I bet you never expected I'd quote Donald Rumsfeld. But one must learn from all directions.

Today's landscape is qualitatively and quantitatively different from that of past civilizations in two ways. First, technology shapes both our world *and* our experience of it—*we have the information*—and, second, we are depleting many of our resources just as the next billion people are entering the middle class. Earth's population is 7 billion and growing. The scientific assessment of this situation paints a very dire picture. Reporters have covered the threat in every kind of media—science, business, policy, religion, lifestyle and sports—for many years now. But ten years after Mr. Rumsfeld's quote, we still have no idea what's coming.

PwC and KPMG began attributing financial costs of environmental destruction to specific corporations and sectors in recent years. On a broader scale, Nicholas Stern, a renowned economist and professor at the London School of Economics, worked with a team at the United Kingdom Ministry of Treasury to issue the Stern Review Report on the Economics of Climate Change in 2006.[12] This controversial document asserts that fighting climate change would cost 1 percent of global gross domestic product (GDP). The cost of *not* fighting climate change? Between 5 and 20 percent of GDP in the very near future. The report calls climate change an economic externality.

In 2008, a mere two years after the Stern Review Report was published, he doubled his estimate from 1 percent of GDP to 2 percent because of new scientific evidence and inadequate global action. He wrote: "The problem of climate change involves a fundamental failure of markets: those who damage others by emitting greenhouse gases generally do not pay."[13] In 2013, Stern said, "Looking back, I understand the risks. . . . I got it wrong on climate change—it's far, far worse."

In 2010, Indian banker and economist Pavan Sukhdev, with a global team organized by the United Nations Environment Programme, released "Bridging the Gap: The Economics of Ecosystems and Biodiversity" (known as TEEB 2010 report), which notes: "The invisibility of biodiversity values has often encouraged inefficient use or even destruction of the natural capital that is the foundation of our economies."[14] In a 2012 interview, Sukhdev asked the perfect question: "When did the bees last send you an invoice for pollination?"

Two examples from TEEB 2010 demonstrate a new way to approach economics and natural systems. First, the total economic value of insect pollination worldwide was estimated in 2005 at

€153 billion, representing 9.5 percent of world agricultural out-put. And second, halving deforestation rates by 2030 would re-duce global greenhouse gas emissions enough to avoid damage from climate change estimated at more than $3.7 trillion. This fig-ure does not even include the many benefits of forest ecosystems.

One can argue with Stern's and Sukhdev's final numbers, just as one can argue with those in the Puma report and early KPMG estimates. But these authors are all ahead of the curve just by developing the language of unified/integrated financial reporting. Only with a unified financial report can business and government assume their rightful roles for twenty-first-century commerce.

The Future of Financial Reporting

There have actually been calls to incorporate natural resources into accounting for several decades. Since at least 1990, academic, governmental and institutional reports from China, Canada, Aus-tralia, Europe, the United States and India have emphasized the necessity of doing so.

Some version of integrated reporting has been in the works since the Technical University in Denmark performed a life cycle assessment for Danish Steel Works in 1991. And in 1995, the Danish government financed the "Annual Environmental Report: Measuring and Reporting Environmental Performance." The re-port, prepared by Price Waterhouse, aimed at setting the account-ing rules for the new field of environmental reporting.[15]

In 2002, the Danish Financial Statements Act was passed, de-manding that companies report on environmental and knowledge management issues that could affect understanding of the compa-nies' financial situation. The Danish companies Novozymes and Novo Nordisk went even further by combining their sustainabil-ity and financial reports into the world's first integrated reports, in 2002 and 2003, respectively.[16]

These Danish initiatives inspired a 2009 revamp of South Africa's Governance Code, which recommended that companies produce an integrated report. The so-called King Code requires that all companies publicly listed on the Johannesburg Stock Exchange produce integrated reports starting in 2010.

Helle Bank Jorgensen, a pioneer of sustainability and integrated reporting (she co-created the first-ever integrated report for Novozymes) and former partner of sustainability at PwC, wrote to me:

> A lot of good work around integrated reporting and accounting standards has seen the light. We see fantastic commitment and energy from companies, business schools, IIRC [International Integrated Reporting Council], GRI [Global Reporting Initiative], the Big 4 (PwC, Ernst &Young, KPMG & Deloitte) as well as a lot of others to get to the 21st century (and beyond) accounting system. I believe that accounting must support and enforce a new kind of relationship between financial and ecological systems. This new vision would incentivize companies and stakeholders to favor commerce that provides the most value for both the economic and environmental landscape.

Today, these efforts have coalesced into a few groups that lead the efforts to integrate environmental and social costs into accounting standards: these groups include GRI, the IIRC, the United Nations Environment Programme—Finance Initiative (UNEP—FI) and a few others. I call the leaders of these groups "revolutionaries in suits." If you doubt that a bunch of accountants could inspire you, attend a conference of one of these groups; I promise you'll be surprised. Their missions may sound a bit dry, but they hold the keys to creating the policies that will allow— actually, demand—that businesses make money while respecting the environment, its assets and its limitations.

GRI's mission includes "the mainstreaming of disclosure on environmental, social and governance performance."[17] Sounds dull, but it's not! And GRI's board and stakeholders include representatives from the senior levels of most of the world's leading financial service firms. Several organizations work alongside GRI, such as the IIRC, CERES, UNEP-FI and the Prince Charles Trust. Strategic alliances include the Organization for Economic Cooperation and Development, UNEP, the UN Global Compact as well as the International Organization for Standardization, whose mission is to "create global standards for business, government and society."[18]

The GRI focuses on social and environmental costs, while the IIRC works across all reporting arenas. Both represent a powerful group of actors.

In 2012, IIRC's website states:

The last few years has seen the worst financial crisis since the 1930s—a crisis that was in part driven by individuals and organizations focusing on short-term profits and rewards irrespective of their long-term sustainability. . . . The crisis has demonstrated the need for capital market decision-making to reflect long-term considerations and has called into question the extent to which corporate reporting disclosures, as they exist today, highlight systematic risks to business sufficiently. Integrated Reporting will provide an important step for organizations facing the challenges of the 21st century.

Hans Hoogervorst, chairman of the International Accounting Standards Board, states: "The concept of integrated reporting is coming of age, and I am delighted to support this initiative."[19]

Together these groups are waging a heroic battle on behalf of the very future of commerce. And many of them have been working this terrain for twenty years and more.

These visionaries must be armed with a new set of rules to guide their clients in the right direction. No consultant or company in the world wants to antagonize or challenge its clients—their two priorities are to do a great job and get their contracts renewed. That's why government participation is essential in enabling—and, where appropriate, mandating—the transition to the new twenty-first-century accounting standards.

Connecting Private Industry with Public Policy

Although accountants hold the crucial intellectual capital to design the new financial framework, they need some courageous financial regulators and politicians as partners in this endeavor. That's why the third pillar of the NMB Framework is that government's role in crafting smart policy is crucial to both incentivizing clean growth and penalizing environmentally dangerous business activity. I never thought I would say this, but in my experience, courage is much more likely to be found among corporate leaders than in the halls of any government—local, federal or international.

Two examples of government's capitulation to foolhardy and shortsighted business lobbying include the repudiation of Brooksley Born and the rejection of Elizabeth Warren's proposals to fix pieces of the financial system. Brooksley Born warned of the destructive potential of unregulated derivatives markets soon after taking the helm of the Consumer Financial Trade Commission in 1994. Every business in the business of derivatives rallied against her and her policies, claiming they would stifle the nation's financial innovation, and President Clinton's other economic advisors sided with the business community. As we now know, Ms. Born was not only right, she was painfully right. The shortsightedness and greed of these companies were central causes of the world's recent financial meltdown. These financial institutions wittingly risked the stability of the entire world economy in order to make short-term profits. Yet the government was not courageous and clear-headed enough to stop them when it had the chance.

In 2008, Elizabeth Warren was appointed chair of the Congressional Oversight Panel to help reestablish a modicum of stability and create new regulations for the financial system. She too was stymied by business lobbyists and politicians unwilling to heed her warnings. Her commonsense approach was so abhorrent to the financial industry that it successfully lobbied against her appointment. As the new Massachusetts senator on the Banking Committee, Warren's first hearing became a viral YouTube hit as she chastised regulators.

As these two government advisors know well, speaking in clear sentences that attribute real profit and loss to real financial transactions does not make you popular in the halls of government. It is worth noting that several of the businesses that lobbied against these two women and their proposed financial reforms have either gone out of business or been sold at fire sale prices, including Countrywide, Lehman Brothers, Bear Stearns, Fannie Mae, Freddie Mac, Washington Mutual, Wachovia, AIG and literally dozens of regional commercial banks. Others may be bankrupt or severely diminished by the time you read these words.

The leveraging of assets by the financial industry without sufficient collateral is completely analogous to environmentally unsafe investments that use resources faster than the earth can replenish them. These natural resources are our ultimate collateral. This is why KPMG's recent report measuring the true cost and value of natural resources is such an important tool for anyone interested in good business and good policy.

In January 2010, the U.S. Securities and Exchange Commission (SEC) took its first step on this road, issuing a new rule stating that corporations need to incorporate the liability from climate change into their 10-Ks (the required comprehensive annual financial reports). Although the ruling was unclear at best, it indicated a nascent trend toward restating and repricing climate risk, even in the United States. Specifically, in the SEC's interpretive guidance (excerpted next), the following areas are shown as examples of where climate change may trigger required disclosure of financial risk.

> *Impact of Legislation and Regulation.* When assessing potential disclosure obligations, a company should consider whether the impact of certain existing laws and regulations regarding climate change is material. In certain circumstances, a company should also evaluate the potential impact of pending legislation and regulation related to this topic.

> *Impact of International Accords.* A company should consider, and disclose when material, the risks or effects on its business of international accords and treaties relating to climate change.

> *Indirect Consequences of Regulation or Business Trends.* Legal, technological, political and scientific developments regarding climate change may create new opportunities or risks for companies. For instance, a company may face decreased demand for goods that produce significant greenhouse gas emissions or increased demand for goods that result in lower emissions than competing products. As such, a company should consider, for disclosure purposes, the actual or potential indirect consequences it may face due to climate change related regulatory or business trends.

> *Physical Impacts of Climate Change.* Companies should also evaluate for disclosure purposes the actual and potential material impacts of environmental matters on their business.[20]

This SEC ruling is a somewhat vague starting point. But over the next few years, with the persistence of the new accounting pioneers, it will be implemented, interpreted and finessed to have bite and clarity. It could have tremendous impact on a variety of industries and their suppliers. The faster a company adapts to these new rules, the less onerous the consequences on its long-term stability.

Two prime examples of bad business betting that the SEC will not get serious on implementing these climate change rules are Ambre Energy and Peabody Energy. Both are pushing for coal ports to be built on the West Coast of the United States. Should these ports be developed, their risk profile is extremely high because their primary client (coal) represents the largest piece of the global warming pie. Creation of these ports would be high risk financially and incur huge environmental debt. Shell and Chevron want to import tar sands oil from Canada through the United States via the Keystone Pipeline. These tar sands are the most carbon-intensive oil deposits in the world. Also, extracting oil from the sands, transporting and refining it are all hugely expensive undertakings. But in addition, SEC regulatory penalties can (and should) apply. Both of these huge fossil fuel infrastructure decisions lock us into fifty years of high greenhouse-gas energy development when there are better, cheaper and cleaner options available.

Conversely, if Microsoft, Google, Apple and Facebook continue to increase their renewable energy development, they should receive benefits from the SEC regulatory system. It is essential that all penalizing regulations also include incentivizing regulations.

Conclusion

Creating new definitions of cost and profit is a truly difficult task. We cannot change these rules overnight because doing so would upend the entire economic system. But we cannot *not* change the rules. That's why a transition agenda is crucial. As corporations begin to extricate themselves from their current societal roles and financial models, we must avoid financial carnage wherever possible. We must empower both brave businesspeople and government officials to help create a framework for twenty-first-century commerce that is relevant to today's world—a world where companies earn true profits. But no one can pretend this transition will be a cakewalk.

I asked Al Halvorsen of PepsiCo what would happen if an accelerated depreciation or a longer-term accounting position provided incentives to make large infrastructure investments that save water, waste and energy. Al replied, "If the financial system offered the incentives, PepsiCo would *only* build state-of-the-art facilities." This is why we need the NMB Framework—to provide financial security as businesses incorporate environmental protection into every decision and investment. Many businesses want to move on this track; they just need better rules.

The Puma EP&L is an early template, and the many groups working to create an integrated reporting system are all encouraging signs for the new accounting standards. But until governments get serious with both incentives for clean growth and penalties for pollution, nothing will change at a speed commensurate with the urgency of our environmental problems.

We know the names of Sumeria and Venice because their civilizations altered the course of history. Today, the world is shifting under our feet yet again. No one knows where or how we will land, but it's clear that we must heed the lessons of the past and create the next revolution in financial reporting. The financial services industry has begun leading this effort, and governments must follow suit as if our lives depended on it—because they do.

4

COURAGE

HIGH RISK, HIGH REWARD

I knew someone had to take the first step and I made up my mind not to move.

—Rosa Parks

As with everything worthwhile, real change only occurs when individuals stick their necks out, break some proverbial balls and lead. This is never easy. Environmental activists have often demonstrated great creativity in highlighting environmental problems. But only in recent years have they been joined by equally strong corporate counterparts demonstrating their own brand of creative leadership. One courageous individual can sound the alarm, but several courageous individuals, backed by big business, big government or a big social uprising, can alter the course of history—for better or for worse.

When the companies discussed in this chapter faced stark environmental problems, each responded appropriately only because one or more of its people rocked the boat. The resulting changes are now viewed as assets to their respective corporation's growth, market position, supply chain management, innovation, brand position and long-term security. But that wasn't at all clear when these brave businesspeople began pushing the rock up the hill. Also highlighted is a story of the U.S. government showing leadership in groundbreaking environmental legislation.

Here are a few inspiring stories from McDonald's, Tiffany's, Walmart, Unilever, Coca-Cola and PepsiCo. There are dozens more examples of companies and individuals stepping out of their comfort zones, but only a few where wholesale change was achieved. Also, the government leadership that led to the Clean Air Act of 1970 is unimaginable today.

If Senators Ed Muskie (D-ME) and Howard Baker (R-TN) had not had the courage of their convictions and the willingness to create legislation that heeded the current scientific data of their day, the air in American cities would be worse than the air in Chinese cities today. These stories do not show the endpoint of any big changes, but rather the gumption and intelligence needed to begin the transformation of our economy.

Good corporate and government policy are worth fighting for!

Forests and McDonald's

In addition to their indescribable beauty, forests provide the planet with 20 percent of its oxygen, and their trees and other foliage absorb carbon dioxide. (Forests sometimes are inelegantly referred to as carbon sinks.) Rain forests alone house 50 percent of Earth's species. Without healthy forests, the world's biodiversity suffers, and creatures great and small disappear. The food chain mutates into a paradise for insects and disease (no creatures to eat and constrain them), and water sources are tainted because there are no intact forests to filter them. Topsoil disappears because there are no trees and other flora to keep it intact. This leads to loss of agricultural land, healthy streams for fish and a greater potential for catastrophic flooding. Perhaps most important, the air becomes too unhealthy to breathe. No matter how you figure it, the consequences of deforestation are horrific.

NO FORESTS, NO LIVABLE PLANET

For most of us in North America and Europe, visiting a virgin forest is a rare and exciting experience. Forests have been cleared and cut at an extremely rapid rate over the last five hundred years, and even where there are large swaths in North America (there are hardly any left in Europe), most are second or third growth. These are still beautiful and sometimes even well managed, but in a forest that has never been cut, the difference is palpable for every sense: sight, smell, sound and touch.

In the Amazon, virgin rain forest still exists, but it is endangered because it is not priced according to its true value. Parts of the Amazon are regularly cleared to grow soybeans for animal feed, raise cattle for leather and hamburgers or build roads and rail lines to access mines. Its managed areas are used to produce sturdy and colorful hardwoods for building, but they are now largely illegal to export. The Amazon also offers cheap land and labor, lax laws and/or lax law enforcement and the agricultural fertility that brought forth its great forests in the first place.

Even so, today many corporations have policies that preclude using products from newly cleared rain forests. Most of these were adopted as a result of hard-fought campaigns by local activists and a variety of national and international nongovernmental organizations (NGOs). Although they are often not stringent enough and are largely unenforced, they do exist. McDonald's is one company that has such a policy.

The Amazon is the largest rain forest remaining on the planet. It spans nine countries, and although famous as a major carbon inhaler, according to the Union of Concerned Scientists, fires used to clear the Amazon accounted for 6 percent of the world's carbon dioxide emissions in 2009.[1] That makes it an exhaler instead.

In April 2006, Greenpeace Amazon confirmed that Cargill, the agribusiness giant and the largest purveyor of soybeans in the world, was clear-cutting huge tracts of the rain forest to build soybeans farms and published the findings in a report titled "Eating Up the Amazon."[2] McDonald's, a major Cargill customer, used this soy to feed the chickens it raises for Chicken McNuggets. Cargill, in 2006 the world's largest privately owned company, had a low public profile, which made it hard for Greenpeace to exert any real pressure on it through shareholders or a public campaign. Nevertheless, in May of that year, Greenpeace activists demonstrated against Cargill all across Europe. They dumped four tons of soy at the entrance to Cargill's European headquarters in the United Kingdom, closed down a chicken processing

Greenpeace blocking the Cargill port in Santarem, Brazil.

Photo by Daniel Beltrá/Greenpeace

plant in France and shut down Cargill's soy export facility in Santarem, Brazil.

Cargill asserted that it was following Brazilian law. On May 1, 2006, the company issued a formal response to the Greenpeace Amazon report that stated: "Economic development is the long-term solution to protecting both the Amazon's peoples and the environment: poverty does not do that. In recognizing the need for an appropriate balance, the Brazilian government has wisely chosen to not prohibit soy production in the forested areas of the Amazon. Instead, Brazil's Forest Code seeks to combine strong environmental protection with limited, but economically important, agricultural production."[3]

Brazil's forest code clearly did *not* take the long view but instead provided incentives for destroying the country's natural resources. The complexity of economic development in industrializing economies makes all three tenets of the NMB Framework

Land in Gleba do Pacoval, 62 miles from Santarem, Amazon, illegally logged to clear land for soya plantations in 2006.

Photo by Daniel Beltrá/Greenpeace

even more crucial, to ensure that short-term gains are not achieved at the expense of midterm financial and environmental security.

Cargill's public profile took a hit, but the company is less vulnerable than McDonald's, whose brand protection and profile are the very keys to its profitability. So even though McDonald's only uses one quarter of 1 percent of the soy grown in the Amazon, Greenpeace began targeting McDonald's in April 2006 for its use of soy from newly deforested Amazon lands. McDonald's already had a 1989 policy in place that read: "Tropical rainforests play an important role in the Earth's ecology. For the record, NOWHERE IN THE WORLD DOES MCDONALD'S PURCHASE BEEF RAISED ON RAIN-FOREST (OR RECENTLY-DEFORESTED) RAINFOREST LAND."[4]

Bob Langert, McDonald's vice president of corporate social responsibility, was the man tasked with responding to the Greenpeace allegations. Even though Greenpeace was still vehemently protesting Cargill during this period, Bob summarized his response to Greenpeace in a 2012 interview. "We agree with you.

Greenpeace protesting McDonald's in Europe.

Photo by Jiri Rezac/Greenpeace

So, now what do you want to do about it? You can't just be targeting McDonald's alone. This is a larger issue."[5]

To me, that was the right answer.

Bob then took a few steps outside the usual corporate VP handbook. First, he checked with supplier Cargill, which contended that it complied with Amazon law, and then with NGOs Conservation International (CI) and World Wildlife Fund (WWF) to confirm the Greenpeace report. The two NGOs confirmed the Greenpeace allegations, and Bob immediately decided to honor the company's beef policy for its soy supply chain as well.

Perhaps McDonald's biggest decision was whether or not to work with Greenpeace at all. Greenpeace had a similar internal debate about working with the world's largest fast food chain. Bob asserted there was no other way forward, given what Greenpeace had disclosed about the Amazon soy supply chain. So, despite his distaste for Greenpeace's harsh attack style and its one-and-a-half pages of demands, Bob Langert stuck his neck out and advocated for a collaborative approach. To this day, he credits his McDonald's colleagues and even Cargill, but it was Bob who made the end result possible.

Bob summed up his thinking to me very clearly: "Odd couples can add to out-of-the-box thinking that leads to innovative win-win scenarios."

Bob remembers meeting with Greenpeace, McDonald's Europe and McDonald's Brazil three times in three weeks, mostly in far-flung conference rooms and airports. All parties agreed to a moratorium on the growth and export of soy from newly deforested Amazon land. As I have often experienced when working with corporate managers, there comes a moment when they understand that they can actually use their corporation's power, muscle and networks to make a big positive impact on the world—and they get almost giddy. In this case, McDonald's executives realized that they could protect a crucial piece of the world's ecology by leading the charge for a wholesale industry transformation on soy. By the second meeting, Bob recalls, he could tell that both sides had decided the ends would justify the means—in this case, cooperation between once archenemies.

McDonald's and Greenpeace became like an entrepreneurial team in a Silicon Valley start-up. Bob described these meetings to me with relish. "Someone would say: 'I know who to call at Marks & Spencer who might be willing to talk.' 'Oh, I know someone at ASDA [Walmart's British arm].'" He described a group of Greenpeace activists and McDonald's senior executives strategizing over phone calls as if they were a guerrilla marketing team.

Thus was the road to a solution paved, and by May—within a month of the April 2006 protests—Frank Muschetto, McDonald's senior vice president of worldwide supply chain, called Cargill and asked it to be part of the solution. Cargill was even more hesitant than McDonald's about working with Greenpeace—after all, demonstrations against Cargill were still ongoing. But Cargill was also being pressured by retail U.K. customers Marks & Spencer, Waitrose and ASDA to change its Amazon policies. Cargill eventually joined in and began calling its rivals to join the moratorium.

On July 25, 2006, a mere three and a half months after the initial Greenpeace report and protests, McDonald's and Greenpeace announced a two-year moratorium on the sale of soy from newly deforested Amazon lands. The agreement included all five major soy producers: Cargill, Archer Daniels Midland, Bunge, Amaggi and Dreyfus as well as Marks & Spencer, Waitrose and ASDA. The moratorium, which has been extended numerous times, is still in place.

Bob Langert didn't hesitate to do the right thing when the facts were in front of him. And he has worked with Greenpeace Amazon to further this moratorium ever since. In 2007, Bob took a nine-day trip up the Amazon, and when he talks about it, it is clear that it left an imprint on him—just as his courage continues to leave an imprint on the Amazon. I hope that the next step for McDonald's is that the company stops selling burgers for a buck, and we stop demanding them.

"When we can make transformative change in supply chain," Bob says, "and it has a trickle effect to other retailers and suppliers, to me that is a lasting legacy."

I couldn't have said it better.

Mining and Tiffany & Co.

Tiffany & Co. and the environmental NGO Earthworks worked together to promote responsibly sourced minerals—from diamonds, to gold, to silver. The story follows multiyear efforts of Tiffany president Mike Kowalski to change mining practices globally.

Mining is as old as the Neanderthals. In Swaziland, a hematite mine has been dated at 45,000 years old, and 5,000 years ago, Native peoples mined copper for tools and weapons in North America while Egyptians mined for copper, gold and turquoise.

Since the Industrial Revolution, mining, like everything else, has undergone a profound transformation. Industrial-scale mines often blow up entire mountaintops to access precious ores, leaving behind holes so big that they can be seen from space. Industrial gold mines that use cyanide to process large quantities of ore (since the late 1960s) sometimes harm whole ecosystems by poisoning waterways and nearby lands with leached metals and acid drainage.

In January 2000, a dam containing toxic waste from the Baia Mare Aurul gold mine in Romania burst, releasing 100,000 cubic meters of cyanide-laden water into the tributaries of Hungary's biggest river, the Tisza. Cyanide is highly toxic, lethal to humans and other species, even in very small doses. The dirty water was carried to the Danube, which flows through Serbia, Bulgaria and Romania. The contamination was measured at one hundred times the limit for safe drinking water.[6]

This mining disaster killed at least 80 percent of the fish in a large swath of the region's waterways, diminished the safety of its water to this day and caused known and unknown environmental disease and habitat destruction. (To date there have been no full studies of the long-term effects.) Yet the owners of the mining operation paid only one nearby village for any damages. The European Union paid for some of the cleanup, and area governments paid for the rest—while, of course, the victims of the pollution are still paying.[7]

This same narrative plays out on a smaller scale all the time. This is why pollution can no longer be free, and all business rules must incorporate the long term. Following the Baia Mare spill, a voluntary certification system was created, the International Code for Cyanide Management, under the auspices of the United Nations Environment Programme (UNEP).[8] Cyanide producers, financial institutions, regulatory personnel, gold mining companies and environmental advocacy organizations from around the world joined together to develop these standards. No mines using these new protocols have been involved in major mine accidents involving cyanide. But these are voluntary standards, and cheaper production methods that yield gold at lower cost still find their way to market.

NO MANDATORY BEST PRACTICES, NO PRESERVATION OF NONRENEWABLE RESOURCES

Mining is an industry that's essential for so much of what we use and produce and also is hugely destructive for water, air and land, near and far. And as we know from every civilization's history, the bounty inside Earth enriches and advances civilization and technology while also driving humans to rape, pillage and murder. Gangs in the Democratic Republic of Congo today commit gruesome atrocities as they seek to gain control over the country's gold, tantalum, tin, diamond and other mines. According to historians, the Roman legions did the same in their quest to control gold, lead and silver mines throughout their vast empire.[9]

The Rape of the Sabine Women.

Pietro da Cortona, 1627–1629.

Most reputable corporations now do everything in their power to avoid conflict minerals and ores. In Congo today, transparency of supply chains is the goal. However, the black market still persists.

The list on the next page, which shows the industrial uses of Canadian mining, surprised me in its extent.

Evidently we all use the resources from mining. You've probably heard about rare earth minerals and the race to control them. These seventeen minerals include indium for solar cells and screens for TVs, computers and mobile phones, and lanthanum used in hybrid cars.[10]

Batteries (cadmium, lithium, nickel and cobalt)	**Housing construction** (gypsum, clay, limestone, sand and gravel)
Circuitry (gold, copper, aluminum, steel, silver, lead and zinc)	**Hybrid car components** (rare earth elements, including dysprosium, lanthanum, neodymium and samarium)
Computer and television screens (silicon, boron, lead, phosphorus and indium)	**Musical instruments** (copper, silver, steel, nickel, brass, cobalt, iron and aluminum)
Cosmetics and jewelry (gold, diamonds, iron oxide, zinc and titanium dioxide)	**Sports equipment** (graphite, aluminum and titanium)
Electricity (coal and uranium)	**Sun protection and medical ointments** (zinc)
Eyeglasses (limestone, feldspar and soda ash)	**Surgical instruments** (stainless steel)
Fertilizer (phosphate, nitrogen, sulphur and potash)	**Vehicles and tires** (steel, copper, zinc, barium, graphite, sulfur and iodine)

Because of their ubiquity in manufacturing, control of rare earths can cause significant strife. Currently China is the dominant player in the global market. Extracting and refining rare earths can also have major environmental consequences. There has been a wide combination of responses to this, including protests against new mines and refineries.[11] There is a race to both control and find rare earths and their alternatives, as well as to develop new mining protocols for those companies serious about decreasing their impacts. Most hearteningly, new recycling technologies are coming to market that will preempt the need for more mining by reusing already-mined materials.[12]

Since we are not going to relinquish mining and its bounty anytime soon, getting mining to be as clean and responsible as possible is of major importance. This is no small task, and it's not cheap. But it is money well spent.

Earthworks has been pushing companies to clean up their mining operations for over twenty-five years. The group focuses on both environmental and human rights abuses. From 1998 through 2008, the organization was led by Stephen D'Esposito. Steve ended up on an unexpected journey when Mike Kowalski, CEO of Tiffany & Co., called him up one day out of the blue.

Tiffany and Earthworks worked together in the aftermath of the controversy over conflict diamonds in the early 2000s to create a Responsible Gold Mining protocol. Mike Kowalski and Tiffany helped set the gold standard (literally) for mining gold and silver. Here's how they did it.

In the 1990s, environmental and human rights NGOs were railing against destructive mining. Irresponsible mines, large and small, caused serious problems with water pollution, dislocation of local people, cyanide and heavy metal pollution and human rights abuses. These problems occurred from Montana, to Brazil, to Africa.

Mike told me that in the late 1990s, the entire industry was blindsided by the news of so-called blood diamonds—stones that came from war zones, primarily in Africa, where their sales were financing atrocities and other violence. He admitted that it might sound strange now, but at that time, supply chains were not as closely scrutinized as they are today. Manufacturers and retailers focused on securing the materials they needed without much thought to their sources. Also, companies that were mining responsibly weren't getting recognition and were unable to differentiate themselves from the pack. And at that time, Tiffany did not cut and polish its own diamonds. Mike decided to change this policy when he became CEO in 1999.

A business's supply chain is the path all of its goods travel, from source to retail shelves. It includes all manufacturing, logistics, technology and transport, and it is a truly complex thing to organize, especially on a global scale. In recent years, environmental risk has become central to supply chain management and logistics decisions. Many companies are finally figuring this out.

During his tenure at Tiffany, Mike brought production in-house, from sourcing to cutting and polishing. As he explained to me very clearly: "If the entire diamond chain is tainted, Tiffany's could not continue business as usual."

At the same time, in the early 2000s, about a dozen NGOs came together, at the invitation of Earthworks and the global antipoverty group Oxfam, to launch a joint public campaign against destructive mining practices. Each organization looked at mining from a different perspective, so combining their resources and energies made a lot of sense. For example, WWF focused on mining's impact on biodiversity; Amnesty International, on human rights abuses. Earthworks was interested in understanding the practical market obstacles and opportunities. By studying the supply chain and the fact that 80 percent of the world's gold went to manufacture jewelry, Earthworks identified an important leverage point. Jewelers could become partners in calling for better mining practices.

The NGOs decided to start with the high-end retailers since brand sensitivity would make it easier to get the attention of Tiffany and Cartier than J. C. Penney and Walmart. While some wanted to simply protest outside Tiffany stores, Earthworks pushed a strategy of talking first.

As Steve was priming himself to call Tiffany, his phone rang first. An unfamiliar voice said, "Mike Kowalski here, I'm the CEO of Tiffany and we've been doing a risk assessment on gold and we see a big risk in the current state of affairs. I hear you might be able to help us."

Mike had already started researching the best practices of gold mines around the world. As there were no real standards to call upon, he called Earthworks, then running its No Dirty Gold campaign. At that moment, the consortium was just beginning to develop what Steve calls a "framework for responsible mining."

No Dirty Gold campaign logo.

Courtesy of Earthworks

At Mike's insistence, the two men got to know each other before embarking on any joint public activism. But Steve knew immediately that Mike was planning on sticking his neck out. He was determined not only to make fundamental changes to Tiffany's supply chain but to improve the image of the whole industry. He felt it was the right thing to do and also good for business. Tiffany could not afford to have its customers thinking about war crimes or defiled land and water. Tiffany is about celebration and pleasure and memorializing love. And it wasn't just Mike's opinion. Customers were already letting management know that blood diamonds and Tiffany made a very bad combination. Mike explained to me that Tiffany had to keep Holly Golightly's promise from the movie *Breakfast at Tiffany's*: "Nothing very bad could happen to you there." That is the essence of the brand.

In 2003, Mike invited the CEOs of a number of leading global mining companies to a series of dinners with himself and Steve. Mike recognized that many were working at making improvements, but he wanted to stress how much more needed to be done. He also knew that to succeed, mining companies needed a business case to justify their investments. He urged each of them to push forward and differentiate themselves from the laggards in the mining sector that were besmirching the industry's reputation. Tiffany was putting skin in the game by changing its own supply chain—to source directly from responsible mines. Mike, Steve and the mining executives began to design solutions and standards to protect their reputations.

In the end, Mike's forceful personality and Tiffany's brand power, if not its market share, held sway. The mining execs agreed to spend a lot of money, change many protocols and practices and develop systems that gained traction with other companies throughout the mid-2000s. Their foresight was rewarded when, a couple of years later, Walmart joined the program and began to push for the same best practices in its supply chain.

Mike also did something way outside the standard job description of a CEO of Tiffany. In March 2004, he placed a full-page ad in the *Washington Post:* Tiffany was publicly opposing bad mining development and urging the United States Forest Service to deny a permit for the proposed Rock Creek Mine in Montana, which was about to be approved.[13]

Everything about this ad was classy, à la Tiffany, but it made the Bush administration really mad because it questioned the permitting of a mine under federal jurisdiction. Figuring that it would likely include some big Republicans, I asked Mike if his board of directors was upset. He said not a one. They understood that a letter like this fundamentally protected the brand and the business. And when he told me he didn't even think of showing the ad to his board before he ran it, I was agog. I cannot imagine

TIFFANY & CO.

To: Dale Bosworth
Chief, U.S. Forest Service

Re: Preserving the Cabinet Mountains Wilderness

Dear Mr. Bosworth:

Given your previous assignment as Regional Forester in northern Montana, you know well the stark beauty of the Cabinet Mountains Wilderness area, a distinctive precinct of the Kootenai National Forest. You are also familiar with the dispute over a plan to allow construction of a mine that would dig three miles of tunnels under those mountains so that copper and silver could be extracted over three decades.

Forest Service officials in the region have approved the Rock Creek project in concept despite vehement opposition by a coalition of local, regional and national conservation groups, along with local business representatives, public officials and ordinary citizens. The opponents' fears are justified.

This huge mine would discharge millions of gallons of waste water per day conveying pollutants to the Clark Fork River and ultimately into Lake Pend Oreille in Idaho, a national treasure in its own right. Vast quantities of mine tailings—a polite term for toxic sludge—would be stored in a holding facility of questionable durability. Wildlife already struggling to survive would face new perils.

Other disputes of this nature, involving public lands administered by the Forest Service or the Bureau of Land Management, are too often settled in favor of developers because statutes and departmental regulations tilt that way. The 1872 General Mining Act is a particularly egregious example. Enacted to encourage rapid development of sparsely settled regions at a very different stage in American history, this obsolete law virtually gives away public lands and the minerals under them to private interests. It remains a perverse incentive for mining in wilderness areas, near scenic watersheds, around important cold water fisheries, and in other fragile ecosystems—all of which are inappropriate for mineral development.

The Rock Creek proposal still faces some regulatory hurdles, as well as legal challenges in both state and federal courts. As the process unfolds, Rock Creek may well become an important icon in what I hope will be a growing national debate over responsible mining policies. That debate must take into account the reality that public land has multiple uses, and some of our most significant land should be protected from mining. This precious real estate should be available to Americans with diverse interests including hunting, fishing and hiking in unspoiled areas.

We at Tiffany & Co. understand that mining must remain an important industry. But like some other businesses benefiting from trade in precious metals, we also believe that reforms are urgently needed. Minerals should—and can—be extracted, processed and used in ways that are environmentally and socially responsible. Government and industry each has a role to play in shaping sensible measures to achieve this goal.

As this effort goes forward, I hope that we can look to the Forest Service and its sister Federal agencies for cooperation. Three years ago, you told the House subcommittee, "The Forest Service should be judged by how we leave the land. . .." All of us who have any influence on how public lands are used should be judged by the same criterion.

Michael J. Kowalski

Michael J. Kowalski
Chairman of the Board and
Chief Executive Officer
March 24, 2004

Tiffany ad that appeared in the Washington Post, 2004. Courtesy Tiffany & Co.

a CEO today not conferring with his or her board before brazenly challenging a controversial government decision.

A spokesperson for the National Mining Association fired back. (Mike's actual words to me were "All hell broke loose.") He accused Mike of putting forth a radical environmental agenda using the bully pulpit of Tiffany. But Steve D'Esposito describes Mike Kowalski as steady and resolute in the face of all this blow-back; he was determined to move his industry and its suppliers toward some fundamental reform. This controversy also showed that there were leaders in the mining sector who also wanted to make progress. Not everyone in the industry attacked the ad—differences began to emerge. And in October 2012, eight years after the Tiffany ad, the Montana Supreme Court voided a key water quality permit for the Rock Creek Mine, so it is not yet operational, if it will ever be.

Ultimately, Mike endorsed the Earthworks Golden Rules for mining companies. In his view, the rules are a core piece of the Tiffany brand. The Golden Rules are:

- Respect basic human rights outlined in international conventions and law.
- Obtain the free, prior and informed consent of affected communities.
- Respect workers' rights and labor standards.
- Ensure that operations are not located in areas of armed or militarized conflict.
- Ensure that projects do not force communities off their lands.
- Ensure that projects are not located in protected areas, fragile ecosystems or other areas of high conservation or ecological value.
- Refrain from dumping mine wastes into the ocean, rivers, lakes or streams.
- Ensure that projects do not contaminate water, soil or air with sulfuric acid drainage or other toxic chemicals.

- Cover all costs of closing down and cleaning up mine sites.
- Fully disclose information about social and environmental effects of projects.
- Allow independent verification of the above.[14]

Today, Tiffany sources all of its gold and silver from the Bingham Canyon Mine, which is owned by mining giant Rio Tinto and sits near Salt Lake City, Utah. Bingham Canyon, mainly a copper mine, is so large it is one of only two man-made items visible from space—the other being the Great Wall of China. Gold is a by-product of its copper operations, and this mine also has its own host of very severe critics, including Earthworks. Bingham Canyon has even been proposed for listing as a Superfund site (the worst hazardous waste problems in the United States). The ore is refined under Tiffany supervision in New England, and Mike stands proudly for the company's entire gold supply chain. Tiffany continues to be a public advocate for leaving certain areas untouched (e.g., Bristol Bay in Alaska) as well as strong protocols for responsible mining.

Years later, we can look back on Mike Kowalski's leadership during this period and see how it has catalyzed change in the mining sector. The mining industry still has enormous challenges before it can be called sustainable. But much of the industry has embraced new protocols and standards, and in August 2012, the U.S. Securities and Exchange Commission issued a ruling that requires companies to trace and audit their supply chain for minerals. Mike Kowalski's willingness to put Tiffany on record helped create the momentum for this smart regulation.[15]

Supply Chain and Logistics: Walmart

In 2005, Lee Scott, then CEO of Walmart, and Rob Walton, chairman and scion of the family that owns 40 percent of the company, were invited by Peter Seligmann, president of Conservation International (CI), to tour several diminishing biodiversity centers. None of them could have imagined that these trips to Costa Rica and Madagascar would change the world in such profound ways. (Well, maybe Seligmann did.) Both Walton and Scott were transformed by what they encountered, and they in turn transformed Walmart, with huge ripple effects on consumer goods manufacturing and supply chain management throughout the global economy. Walmart is the third largest company in the world, and its supply chain reaches virtually every corner of the world.

After these trips, Walton joined CI's board of directors and donated $21 million of his own money for ocean protection. But Seligmann saved his biggest ask for Walmart itself. He proposed that Walmart overhaul its entire supply chain, electricity, packaging, transportation and logistics, and use its huge buying power to alter what it stocks on the shelves. Because of Walmart's position as the world's largest retailer, this decision automatically forced thousands of suppliers to change their environmental policies as well. When your biggest purchaser (i.e., Walmart) demands change, you listen very carefully. This was a very smart ask.

Seligmann reflected on his strategy six years later at a 2012 *Fortune* conference:

> We worked with Walmart because Walmart has 100,000 suppliers, and we were going one-offs, company after company, and we thought rather than doing that there's got to be a different way to do this. So, it was if Walmart embraces these concepts and sees that it's good for the customers, it's good for their employees, it's good for reduction of waste, increasing energy efficiency, securing a supply chain, that means it's good for the shareholder. And if you push that down the supply chain and say to your suppliers, you know, best shelf space goes to the best

company, the green one, that really made our work—that was a
global agent of change, and we focused on that.

... This is a big shift, but there's an enormous urgency, too.
I mean, when we look at metrics, we look at population, 7 billion to 9 billion in the next four decades, we're going to double
our demand for energy, food and water, we've got extinction
rates that are accelerating, we've got fisheries that are collaps-
ing, we don't really have time to dillydally.[16]

Many books have been written about Walmart and the consumption paradigm of cheap goods and labor. A $1 plastic toy, a
$20 DVD player and a $25 chaise lounge are all used briefly and
then break. There's nothing inherently sustainable about them—
quite the opposite. It is true that most of the offerings in Walmart
can remain underpriced because they incur huge environmental
debt and are produced in terrible working conditions by people
working for extremely low wages. However, this is not Walmart's
situation alone. This is the conundrum facing the entire global
economy.

Miranda Ballentine, Walmart's director of sustainability, described to me the various internal and external reactions to the
company's surprising embrace of environmental values.

Walmart had, in the early days, and still has today, more opponents than probably any other company on every single topic,
simply due to our scale and visibility, and sustainability is no
different. Sustainability at Walmart has proponents and opponents, and as a result the launch, implementation, and main-
taining momentum took courage and perseverance from our
leadership . . . shareholders have publicly declared Walmart's
leaders as "tree-hugging socialists." On the opposite end of the
spectrum, Walmart receives criticism from people who believe

that a financial benefit to sustainability efforts diminishes the social value of the work.

In 2006, Walmart embarked on a sustainability initiative that rocked the retailing world and developed straightforward aspirational goals—"to be supplied 100 percent by renewable energy; to create zero waste; and to sell products that sustain people and the environment." The company still has a long way to go, and it is not moving as fast as it could, but I would venture that it actually has a shot at achieving its number one goal—using 100 percent renewable energy. The third goal especially—selling "products that sustain people and the environment"—seems unattainable without a revolution in the company's merchandise and pricing structure.

When Walmart measured its carbon footprint in 2006, it discovered that refrigeration was the second largest piece, topped only by the energy used to run the stores. With that in mind, in July 2006, my Greenpeace colleagues Lisa Finaldi, Kert Davies and I visited Walmart headquarters to discuss bringing greener refrigerators into its U.S. stores and trucks.

The first surprise at Walmart headquarters came when we were ushered into a waiting room before our meeting with senior management. It resembled an interrogation room in a *Law & Order* episode. The second surprise was that the waiting room *was* the meeting room. But the biggest surprise was the meeting itself—it was thrilling because the Walmart senior management made clear the company's serious intentions on a wide array of environmental advances.

The day after that meeting, Walmart CEO Lee Scott convened the first Sustainability Initiative summit for all Walmart staff as well as a spectrum of NGOs at headquarters in Bentonville, Arkansas. After the famous Walmart cheers, Scott showed Al Gore's film, *An Inconvenient Truth*, and hosted two speakers—Al

Gore and Rick Cizik, a prominent evangelical environmentalist. This presentation signaled very clearly to all Walmart stakeholders—employees, shareholders and customers—that Lee Scott, the Walton family and Walmart were serious about environmental action. The CEO's deference to such prominent environmentalists empowered employees to push suppliers in ways previously unthinkable.

A few months later, Kert and I were invited back by Alan Epler, then Walmart's small electronics merchandise manager, who had invited his two refrigerator suppliers (GE and Haier) to headquarters. At the request of Walmart, Kert and I invited Coca-Cola representatives. We left that meeting genuinely astonished. The Coca-Cola engineers finished our sentences—in fact, they began our sentences! Imagine a multinational corporation advocating loudly and proudly for a Greenpeace position. Blow me down with a feather. And then Alan Epler said to his two refrigerator suppliers, "OK, who is going to bring me the first green refrigerator to sell in the United States?" Again, blow me down with a feather. I believe that GE began its research and design into this new-to-America technology five minutes after that meeting ended. The refrigerator was finally introduced in 2012.

The Sustainability Initiative's initial burst of energy, inspired by CEO Lee Scott's wake-up call on his trip with Peter Seligmann and Rob Walton, was followed by a string of well-publicized successes, both environmental and financial. In fall 2006, Walmart committed to phasing out the sale of incandescent light bulbs (the round ones we've all been using until recently) for compact fluorescents and announced a very aggressive goal to sell 100 million compact fluorescents by 2008. Walmart surpassed that goal by late 2007.

The light bulb story is always mentioned as a minor improvement in overall efforts to avert catastrophic global warming. It is not minor; it's just that we have so much to do most anything feels too little, too late. We must dismiss this cynicism and instead pursue thousands of similar changes that re-create and redefine other industries, such as energy and agriculture. These industries are much harder to crack. But Walmart is actually working on those too. Here are some light bulb stats.

A fluorescent is eight times more expensive than an incandescent one. It uses 75 percent less electricity, lasts ten times longer and saves a consumer $30 in energy costs over the life of each bulb. In the long view, these newer bulbs are much cheaper despite their eight-times-higher initial cost and the need to recycle the mercury used in their production. Light-emitting diode (LED) technology will likely replace both incandescents and fluorescents in the near future. In 2007, Walmart's fluorescent bulb sales alone saved Americans $3 billion in electricity costs and avoided the building of additional power plants for the equivalent of 450,000 new homes. If pollution were no longer free, incandescent bulbs would cost more because the cost of those extra power plants would be included in their pricing.

Sticking with household goods, Walmart also demanded that its suppliers completely repackage their goods. The company now only sells concentrated liquid laundry detergent, which has saved more than 400 million gallons of water, 95 million pounds of plastic resin, 125 million pounds of cardboard and 520,000 gallons of diesel fuel over the past three years. Smaller packaging costs less to transport. "Lee [Scott] pushed me," said A. G. Lafley, CEO of Procter & Gamble, and "we totally, totally changed the way we manufacture liquid laundry detergents in the U.S. and, now, around the world."[17] These are all important improvements, yet they are still a long way from Walmart's goal of selling products that "sustain people and the environment." After all, the ingredients in most of these products still contain dangerous chemicals that harm air, land and sea.

By March 2011, Walmart had achieved its goal of 80 percent less waste going to landfills from its California operations. The company acknowledges that "achieving a similar 80 percent reduction in its landfill waste across the country would help Walmart prevent more than 11.8 million metric tons of carbon dioxide emissions annually. This is equal to taking more than 2 million cars off the road for a year."[18] These statistics underscore the huge amount of greenhouse gas emissions Walmart produces annually and why the company must be even more aggressive in its waste reduction programs.

Walmart makes it easy to both love and hate it. In 2011, it stood with Greenpeace and WWF against a giant paper corporation. The two environmental NGOs were launching public campaigns to keep Asian Pulp & Paper's (APP) products out of the United States because of the company's terrible deforestation policies. Billionaire oil barons the Koch Brothers' advocacy organization, the Consumers Alliance for Global Prosperity, generated thousands of letters asking Walmart to adamantly oppose the two environmental organizations, and several politicians actively lobbied Walmart to support APP's U.S. subsidiaries. Miranda Ballentine wrote to me: "Walmart stood our ground in actively opposing APP products in the U.S. supply chain—not in defense of Greenpeace or WWF—but because we felt it was the right choice for our customers and their children's future." The company's courage is as surprising as it is impressive.

Regarding its aim to reduce overall packaging and transport costs, just by redesigning its trucks and loading them more efficiently, Walmart has seen a 25 percent improvement in fuel efficiency. The company estimates it will save nearly $500 million a year in fuel costs by 2020 by this simple change. Less fuel, lower carbon emissions.

And now it is even moving into renewable energy. As of 2010, Walmart was the second-largest onsite green power generator in the United States. The company has 180 renewable energy projects in operation or under development, and it continues to test solar, fuel cells, microwind and offshore wind. If governments provided incentives and coordinated the numerous private efforts at energy development—the role government should play—Walmart's efforts in renewable energy could be leveraged to help build a renewable electricity grid.

And the piece of Walmart's greening that is more complex but potentially has the highest impact is just coming on line in 2012: its "Integrated Sustainability Index." In the company's own words: "This new retail tool will assess and improve the sustainability of our products. . . . Over the last year, we used these metrics to develop our first category scorecards to help our buyers evaluate products, and we expect to develop scorecards in up to 100 major categories by the end of 2012."[19]

In plain English, this means that if your products are not made with state-of-the-art, sustainable manufacturing and sourcing, Walmart will not stock them. This is a game changer for the world's manufacturers of pretty much everything because Walmart is almost everyone's largest customer.

In agriculture, as of 2008, Walmart was the largest purveyor of organic milk and organic cotton in the United States, and the reliability of those purchasing agreements means that organic agriculture can invest and grow as it must. The company has also committed $1 billion a year to purchase produce from 1 million small and medium farms worldwide. In fact, 10 percent of all produce sold in Walmart's U.S. stores is purchased from local (in-state) farms.

As much as I love the sensibility of my local green market or natural food store, it takes Walmart's scale of purchasing power to provide organic agricultural pioneers a large enough market share to go mainstream. And small farmers need dependable revenue to survive. (Walmart's organic standards are lower than those of a local green market—for example, most of its organic milk is not from free-range or grass-fed cows.) And the vast majority of the milk Walmart sells remains full of hormones and antibiotics.

The company's sustainability initiative faced some stiff opposition. Skeptics said it would cost too much money, take too much time, divert staff from growth and, overall, it would not be a fit for Walmart's market niche—cheap and easy. None of this stopped Lee Scott and Rob Walton from moving their company to embrace new ways of doing business. There's still a long way to go, but if bravery and backbone count for anything, they'll get there.

Connecting Private Ambition with Public Policy: Unilever

Have you heard? Money influences public policy. The rules that govern, subsidize, penalize, incentivize, regulate, tax and insure business can determine what is profitable and what is not.

And everything from subsidies and price supports for large soy growers, to the cost of rights to drill for oil or gas on national lands, to the posting of flood insurance for real estate development on floodplains, to the ability to trade on margin using funds guaranteed by the government is there to be lobbied for or against by the groups that stand to benefit.

Government policy frames most aspects of our economy. The idea that there is a free market is largely a myth. If it's my business that is getting the policy perks and tax breaks, I'm likely to call it "free." If only your business is getting these perks, not so much.

But a few mainstream business institutions are now turning this lobbying on its head. Debates are raging in the hallowed halls of the *Harvard Business Review,* the World Economic Forum, McKinsey & Co. and every other well-heeled business community you can imagine. Some very surprising folks are coming out in support of the "new rules of capitalism."

In March 2011, Dominic Barton, CEO of McKinsey, wrote an essay in the *Harvard Business Review* called "Capitalism for the Long Term" wherein he urged businesses to manage and report around five- to seven-year periods instead of traditional quarterly reports.

Paul Polman, CEO of Unilever, went even further on the *Review*'s website, saying that Barton's prescriptions

will all go a long way to addressing the problems of short-term capitalism. They are necessary. But they are not sufficient. Changes in policy will mean little if not accompanied by changes in behavior. That's why we need a different approach to business—a new model led by a generation of leaders with the mind-set and the courage to tackle the challenges of the future. Such challenges go beyond those arising from the financial crisis. We now know, in outline, what the future will look like. It will be a world where climate will change, water will be scarce, and food supplies will be insecure.

Business has a chance to become part of the solution to those challenges. Just as we need to ensure that we do not repeat the mistakes which led to the recent banking crisis, so there is an equal imperative to face up to the realities of a world where 9.5 billion people will put enormous strain on biophysical resources. The rapidly growing populations of India, China, and Indonesia will all aspire to the lifestyles and living standards enjoyed by the Germans and the Californians. There is nothing that we can, or should, do to stop that.

The challenge for business is to meet these needs in a sustainable fashion. Success will require completely new business models. It will demand transformational innovation in product and process technologies to minimize resource use, as well as the development of "closed-loop" systems so that one man's waste becomes another's raw material.[20]

And Polman is actually moving the company he leads to reach for this ambition.

We are all accustomed to private corporations lobbying for laws, rules and regulations that provide subsidies, increase profits, shortcut environmental and social responsibility and, generally, make the rest of us cringe. Unilever, though, has turned this kind of lobbying on its head.

Unilever's Sustainable Living Plan (SLP), introduced in 2010, is so far-reaching that the company realized it would need to push for new regulations and stricter policies in order to reach the plan's fifty stated goals. Instead of lowering its ambitions, it started a global advocacy office that works to change the rules of business in a way that very closely adheres to the NMB Framework where pollution is no longer free, long-term investments are rewarded and governments create incentives for positive environmental and social actions while charging for harmful ones. This newly configured playing field would give all sustainable industries the competitive advantage they sorely need.

Unilever aims to halve its environmental and social impact while simultaneously doubling its business by 2020. Both the sales/sustainability targets and timelines are extremely ambitious. Many companies want to double sales in a decade. But most companies resolve to halve their impacts by 2040 or 2050, giving themselves three or four times the leeway in which to make these big operational changes. Unilever's ten-year timeline is a deliberate device to ensure that the company cannot wait for better economic times or better regulations or some future crisis that demands immediate action. It must move on all fronts today.

For example, in order for Unilever to eliminate 50 percent of its product and manufacturing waste, its Global Advocacy Office is working to increase regulatory pressure on landfill usage and waste production. The company is well aware that the SLP is not sufficient to address the world's environmental problems. All companies must move in the same direction, and that will happen only when public policy changes. In countries with strict garbage and landfill laws that mandate only a certain percentage of waste go into landfills, recycling rates are higher. With stronger laws, the SLP will reach its goal of decreasing half of the company's waste while also forcing other companies to do the same. This is truly a new model of business lobbying.

Another way Unilever is pushing the envelope involves commodities. The company is urging the World Trade Organization to reduce tariffs on agricultural and mineral products that are sourced sustainably. Again, this would present other companies with a new choice: Either pay for the real costs of your existing supply chain or improve it so that racking up environmental debt does not provide a financial advantage. This is the raison d'être of the company's Global Advocacy Office.

Unilever CEO Polman is an outspoken leader who often expounds on the need to reframe the rules of capitalism for the common good. But unlike many other business leaders who might not walk the talk, Polman is embedding this vision into Unilever's entire value chain, internal and external.

Unilever spent much of 2009 devising the fifty goals that would comprise its SLP. As far as I know, no other multinational, publicly traded company has taken sustainability goals and fully incorporated them into basic financial targets and internal performance metrics.

If the personal hygiene division makes a ton of money but fails to reach its sustainability goals, the division is not rewarded; it's put on notice. For example, palm oil is an ingredient in hundreds of Unilever products, and, until 2009, much of the company's supply came from endangered rain forests in Indonesia. Unilever is not only switching its sourcing but working hand in hand with the 400 member companies of the Consumer Goods Forum (CGF) and governments to help scale up alternative sources and practices for all forest products. According to a June 2012 U.S. Agency for International Development press release, "The U.S. Government and the companies of the Consumer Goods Forum are working together to reduce deforestation by promoting sustainable supply chains."[21] The joint release goes on to promote sustainable forestry for palm oil, soy, paper and beef. Production of these four commodities causes 50 percent of global deforestation—in just four countries! Unilever and WWF jointly spearheaded the forum's Deforestation Resolution. The resolution's intentions are no less than to fundamentally change the world's forestry markets and supply chains.

Not surprisingly, the SLP was controversial with employees—many people felt it would stretch the company's resources by demanding too much time, money and energy. Plus, by making the goals public, Unilever opened the door to scrutiny from both civil society stakeholders as well as its shareholders. (Unilever's Ben & Jerry's division might have included such environmental and social metrics in performance evaluations when the company was actually controlled by Ben and Jerry, but Unilever is not a boutique Vermont-based operation; it is a $58 billion global corporation.)

Thomas Lingard, director of Unilever's Global Advocacy Office, explained to me the company's response to these concerns: "If you show to stakeholders and others that you are seriously trying to do something extraordinary, and you don't make it, they are inclined to *help* you reach your goal—not beat you up."

I attended a presentation by Unilever senior management on its 2011 SLP performance. One of the most striking moments occurred during the question-and-answer session. Gavin Neath, then senior vice president of sustainability, was asked how the company was performing in one area of the plan: health and nutrition. He said, "I'd give us a failing grade, and I think we have to concentrate more there." I almost fell off my chair—I had never heard such an honest answer in a corporate presentation before. Neath is leading the company's deforestation work with the CGF.

Examples of the company's goals and its own scoring are shown in the next figures. You can access Unilever's continuing progress at its website.

None of this means that Unilever's products are all nontoxic or good for you or the environment. Look at the next two lists, which contain ingredients for two products, one for use on your body and one to ingest. Can you guess which is which? In fact, most of the ingredients are harmless and are listed by their chemical names rather than their commonly used ones, so they sound much worse than they are. But some of these ingredients ain't so good for you or for the environment. I presume these ingredients will change as the company moves further along its sustainability journey.

Ingredients A

Aqua, Sodium Laureth Sulfate, Sodium C12–13 Pareth Sulfate, Cocamidopropyl Betane, Glycol Distearate, Dimethiconol, Glycerin, Tea-Dodecylbenzenesulfonate, Lauryl Glucoside, Arginine, Panthenol, Hydrogenated Palm Glucoside, Carbomel, Sodium Chloride, Guar Hydroxypropyltrimonium Chloride, Sodium Hydroxide, Citric Acid, Parfum, DMDM Hydantoin

Ingredients B

[first four ingredients excised] Calcium Caseinate, Gum Arabic, Cellulose Gel, Hydrogenated Soybean Oil, Mono and Diglycerides, Potassium Phosphate, Soybean Lecithin, Cellulose Gum, Carrageenan, Isolated Soy Protein, Artificial Flavor, Maltodextrin, Sucralose and Acesulfame (Nonnutritive Sweeteners), Dextrose, Potassium Carrageenan, Citric Acid and Sodium Citrate. Vitamins and Minerals: Magnesium Phosphate, Calcium Phosphate, Sodium Ascorbate, Vitamin E Acetate, Zinc Gluconate, Ferric Orthophosphate, Niacinamide, Calcium Pantothenate,

Working as Unilever in the supply chain

Sometimes acting alone can catalyse change across the industry

 In 2007 we were the first large company to commit to **sustainable sourcing of tea**

Many tea companies have followed us

 In 2008 we committed to draw all of our **palm oil from certified sustainable sources by 2015**

Much of the industry has followed

 We will source all our **cocoa sustainably by 2020**

 Ben & Jerry's are asking Fairtrade to **certify their key ingredients**

 Knorr has established a €1 million **Partnership Fund** to help farmers

 Our **Sustainable Agriculture Code** is an open source document available to our suppliers and others

2011 HIGHLIGHTS

What is left to do

 24% of agricultural raw materials sustainably sourced

– in 2011

Although we have made good progress on our top 10 materials, there remains much to do

 64% of our palm oil now sourced sustainably

– we are on track to meet our 2015 target

The next step is to develop segregated supplies of certified palm oil which can be traced back to the plantations on which they were grown

 48 million people reached with Lifebuoy soap handwashing programmes

over 2010–11

New partnerships will help us scale up further, and our 'train the trainer' approach in Indonesia will be extended

 100% of our electricity purchased in Europe now from renewable sources

– which saves 250,000 tonnes of CO_2 emissions a year

Overall, renewable energy now contributes 20% of our total energy use. We need to double this figure to reach our target of 40%

 Over 90% of our leading spreads contain **less than ⅓ saturated fat**

Tackle the remainder which need higher saturated fat content to stay stable in tropical countries

 35 million people have gained access to safe drinking water from Pureit since 2005

We need to make Pureit available to more low-income consumers. We are working with NGO partners to improve accessibility and affordability

Unilever 2011 Sustainable Living Plan. Courtesy of Unilever

Manganese Sulfate, Vitamin A Palmitate, Pyridoxine Hydro-chloride, Riboflavin, Thiamin Mononitrate, Folic Acid, Chro-mium Chloride, Biotin, Sodium Molybdate, Potassium Iodide, Phylloquinone (Vitamin K1), Sodium Selenite, Cyanocobalamin (Vitamin B12) and Cholecalciferol (Vitamin D3)

Answers: Ingredients A make up Dove Shampoo. Ingredients B are part of Slim-Fast.

As Unilever's Global Advocacy Office pushes for regulations to aid the company's strong environmental and social initiatives, environmental and social policies of all other businesses will be affected. This is one helluva courageous move for a publicly traded company.

Regulation and Policy:
When Only Radical Change Will Suffice

> Our most basic common link is that we all inhabit this small planet. We all breathe the same air. We all cherish our children's future. And we are all mortal."
>
> —John Fitzgerald Kennedy, June 10, 1963

The air in Beijing, Mexico City, Athens, Delhi and many other great world capitals is rife with pollution and poisonous for all living things—even buildings, from the Acropolis to the Taj Mahal, are crumbling. Same goes for the air in China's industrial centers.

American cities also have terrible pollution. In 2010, the Riverside-San Bernardino area of the Los Angeles Basin had 110 smog alert days (one out of every three days with unhealthy air).[22] The American Lung Association notes that half of all Americans live in areas that experience unhealthy levels of smog on a regular basis. Without the revolutionary 1970 Clean Air Act (CAA) and its subsequent amendments, American cities would be in even worse shape than China's, and global warming would be even further along on its trajectory.

Even in the 1950s and 1960s, the air in Los Angeles made people sick, shortened lives and destroyed nearby agriculture. Fifty years later, its greenhouse gas trail continues to contribute to today's global warming by elevating the accumulated carbon dioxide (CO_2) levels in Earth's atmosphere. These facts help to illuminate why we must include long-term effects in all calculations of wealth creation—estimating the future costs of today's actions for the public, private and individual sectors even decades later. That is the policy gauntlet for today's politicians. Will any step up?

I visited Joshua Tree National Park in Southern California in the late 1990s, and I remembered a photo montage showing the degradation of the natural landscape from air pollution. Thanks to the National Park Service for digging it up (it's no longer in the park) and allowing me to reprint it.

Ouch. In the fifty years since President Kennedy's eloquent words, we still have not learned to honor the common link of human survival. Despite the efforts of some extraordinary politicians from the 1970s, we are still pursuing short-term money and convenience over our children's very futures.

Ed Muskie, Howard Baker, and the Clean Air Act of 1970: A History Lesson for a Gridlocked Government

This is a story about a few American senators who listened to science and risked unpopularity to create the template for smart air pollution and water policy. The fact that the legislation has not been enforced well enough or expanded commensurate with exceedingly dire science does not diminish their great accomplishment. Would that today's politicians—globally—follow these men's example.

How did a group of foresighted and brave senators get the landmark 1970 Clean Air Act passed? In short, with courage and

Joshua Tree National Park.

What's Wrong with this Picture?

Mount San Jacinto

Palm Springs

Santa Rosa Mountains

On clear viewing days you can look southwest and see Palm Springs and San Jacinto Peak (10, 831 feet).

Mount San Jacinto

Palm Springs

The answer is haze. Haze comes from such sources as water vapor, dust, and air pollution. Air pollution can come from locations many miles away. Southern California industrial plants, power plants, wood stoves, and automobiles belch soot, dust, and smoke into the atmosphere. Prevailing winds direct the air east and funnel it through Banning Pass, where it is dispersed throughout the Coachella Valley.

Some pollutants that form haze are linked to serious health problems and environmental damage. Occasionally air pollution exceeds national health standards here in the park.

On very hazy days it is difficult to find Palm Springs, 20 miles (32 km) away, nestled at the foot of Mount San Jacinto. The haze hangs around the longest when winds are calm, humidity is high, and temperatures are hot.

Courtesy of the National Park Service

tenacity. Throughout the 1960s, Senate Energy and Commerce Committee chair Ed Muskie took his title seriously, traveling around the United States gathering information on pollution, especially its effects on health. He became convinced of the urgent need for action. Muskie understood the science, the economics and the health impacts behind different kinds of emissions, and his Senate colleagues often deferred to his expertise because he had done his homework for over a decade. And Muskie had a young Republican cohort, Howard Baker, who joined him for this journey. Baker and Muskie, friends since Baker joined the Senate in 1967, became the team that created and championed this radical legislation.

In the 1960s, America, then a major manufacturing center, was in the midst of a visible, palpable pollution crisis. It led to the first Federal Clean Air Act of 1963, which demanded new air quality criteria and clearer research on pollution's scientific and health implications. The government gave grants to state and local districts in an attempt to control pollution, and Muskie attended many of the hearings to learn the issues firsthand. California, in particular, ran with the effort. Los Angeles had experienced its first serious smog episode in 1943 and had already established its Bureau of Smoke Control in 1945. But this early legislation did not change the regulatory paradigm. In 1970, Southern California measured an ozone concentration five times greater than the health-based national standard that would be adopted in 1971.

Muskie's canny political instincts coincided with the early stirrings of the global environmental movement and the first Earth Day in 1970. His lead aide on environmental issues, Leon Billings, explained to me some serendipitous luck. An acute temperature inversion in Washington, D.C., made the air dangerous for several weeks at the same time as committee deliberations on the CAA in 1970. It was Washington's worst air pollution ever, and both Muskie and Baker milked the good timing of this bad situation.

But without the committee's courage to look to the future, the then-radical CAA could not have been created or passed. As it was, General Motors, consumer crusader Ralph Nader and the two senators from Michigan tried to get Leon fired in the course of the deliberations—a healthy set of diverse enemies. Senator Muskie stood firm against the senators from Michigan, even though every vote counted.

And then in 1972, President Nixon used Muskie's environmental work against him. Leon, by then Muskie's chief of staff, explained to me that the Nixon administration feared Muskie as the frontrunner candidate for the 1972 presidential election and used the senator's strong environmental passions to incite voter sentiment against him. Nixon sent a variety of corporate representatives to influential members of the Senate after the CAA came out of committee. Large industries—especially oil, paper and car companies—were just beginning to realize that the Act could actually affect how business was done. These corporate representatives pushed mightily, but somehow Muskie and his staff neutralized the attacks. When Nixon finally, begrudgingly, signed the CAA (at the strong request of Republican Senate leaders), Muskie was not invited to the White House ceremony.

Since then, industry has fought every pollution control law like crazy.

Lee Iacocca, then vice president of Ford Motor Company, called the CAA "a threat to the entire American economy and to every person in America." He added that the emissions standards were "in two words: IM POSSIBLE." As a final comment, he said, "We've got to pause and ask ourselves: How much clean air do we need?"[23]

I think we all know the answer.

NO AIR, NO LIFE

The auto industry became much more organized, fighting future amendments to the CAA, as seen in Mobil and Chrysler ads against the 1973 amendment.[24] Mobil's ad stated that the CAA was a "$66 billion mistake" and Chrysler's ad stated that by 1975 each new car would cost up to $1,300 extra to own and drive. Chrysler noted that the proposed new emissions controls will "1. Go beyond what is necessary to protect our health, 2. Not result in significantly cleaner air, and 3. Will waste both money and natural resources." Remember the 1939 Frank Capra movie *Mr. Smith Goes to Washington?* Jimmy Stewart is the laughingstock of the U.S. Senate as he fights the corrupt political machine and the corporation it represents, but he will not rest (literally) until justice is done. Although now considered a Hollywood classic, the film was originally attacked as anti-American by the sitting senators for its portrayal of government corruption. (An aside I cannot omit here is that Capra wrote and produced a film called *The Unchained Goddess* in 1958, under the auspices of the Bell Laboratory Science Series—the very first television broadcast to describe global warming and its threat to civilization.)

So, how did Senators Ed Muskie and Howard Baker craft such a revolutionary bill? And how did they get it passed? Muskie focused on health, Baker on technology-forcing. And committee member Senator Thomas Eagleton (D) of Missouri ensured that the bill also included deadlines for the required changes. In a 2005 speech to the University of Tennessee, Senator Baker, when he was Ambassador to Japan, described the bill's precedents and passage with inspiring clarity.

> In 1969 Senator Ed Muskie and I came together with a shared vision. We each provided critical elements to that vision and we succeeded in producing a law which more than well demonstrated that the whole is greater than the sum of its parts. Walk with me, if you would, through some of the critical provisions of that law—provisions still working today, most of which were unique and unprecedented in 1970. Before we start down this path, let

me remind each of you that the Clean Air Act of 1970 passed the United States Senate unanimously. Ultimately, the conference report on the Clean Air Act passed the United States Senate unanimously—unanimous, but yet unique and unprecedented.

First and foremost, we declared a direct and overarching federal interest in protecting the health of all Americans from air pollution.

Second, we incorporated in law the concept of technology forcing.

Third, we established deadlines for government action.

Fourth, we made many of those government actions mandatory rather than permissive.

Fifth, we empowered the public, individual American citizens, with the authority to use the federal courts to achieve the objectives we set forth should the bureaucracy or the politicians fail to do so.

To my knowledge, none of these concepts had ever been legislated before. And all were contained in a 38-page—I want to underscore 38-page—public law called the Clean Air Act of 1970.[25]

The Environmental Protection Agency (EPA), in a 2011 white paper requested by Congress, reported that the CAA has cut emissions of the six most widespread pollutants by 60 percent since 1970. This means that in 2010 alone, the CAA prevented 1.7 million instances of worsened asthma, 160,000 premature deaths, 85,000 respiratory and cardiovascular hospital admissions and 54,000 cases of chronic bronchitis. These savings of suffering and death also translate to major financial savings. The EPA noted: "Implementing the Clean Air Act's public health protections would potentially amount to '2.8 percent of total U.S. health care costs.' Total annual savings are estimated to be over $50 billion. Translation? Net economic benefits exceeding $1 trillion in 2010 alone, a number projected to reach $2 trillion by 2020."[26]

Clearly, the CAA saves lives, dollars and untold suffering. If today's sitting senators paid heed to current science on climate change, the United States might have a strong climate bill that taxes carbon emissions. Pollution can no longer be free.

Muskie described the crafting of the 1970 CAA in a 1990 speech to the Environmental Forum celebrating the act's twentieth anniversary.

> Earth Day 1970 helped create the national psyche which molded that result. But a few committed, progressive Senators sitting in a back room in the Dirksen Senate Office Building made the political and intellectual commitment which forced the achievement of that objective. As Earth Day 1990 approaches, we should call the roll of that small band of men who changed history so we don't forget their important contribution! Jennings Randolph, West Virginia. Stephen Young, Ohio. B. Everett Jordan, North Carolina. Birch Bayh, Indiana. Joseph Montoya, New Mexico. William Spong, Virginia. Thomas Eagleton, Missouri. Mike Gravel, Alaska. John Sherman Cooper, Kentucky. J. Caleb Boggs, Delaware. Howard Baker, Tennessee. Robert Dole, Kansas. Edward Gurney, Florida. And Robert Packwood, Oregon.[27]

Yes, indeed, we should thank this group of Democratic and Republican senators. And hope that their inspired leadership moves back into the Capitol building soon.

Climate Change Case Study: F-gases: Coca-Cola, PepsiCo, Unilever, UNEP, and Greenpeace

In 1973, two scientists from the University of California, Irvine, Frank Sherwood Rowland and Mario Molina, hypothesized that a hole was forming in Earth's ozone layer and that it was largely caused by chlorofluorocarbons (CFCs), the most commonly used refrigerant at the time. The chair of the board of DuPont, the world's largest CFC manufacturer, called the ozone depletion theory "a science fiction tale . . . a load of rubbish . . . utter nonsense."[28] Over the next decade, the hypothesis was confirmed by numerous scientists around the world. In 1995, Rowland and Molina won the Nobel Prize in Chemistry for their discovery.[29] Earth's ozone layer absorbs the sun's ultraviolet radiation and thereby protects all living things from getting burned. This essential protection extends from humans, to crops, to phytoplankton.

Despite industry objections, in 1987, the United Nations began gathering signatory countries for a phase-down and eventual phase-out of CFCs, which it called the Montreal Protocol. Within a decade, 197 countries would sign. An early advocate of the Montreal Protocol, Greenpeace launched over a hundred demonstrations around the world to galvanize support for the treaty.

In 1992, when CFCs were clearly on their way out, Honeywell, DuPont, Solvay and other chemical manufacturers introduced hydrofluorocarbons (HFCs) as the "environmental alternative" to the newly banned refrigerants. Unfortunately, they were not the environmental alternative to anything. The new HFCs eliminated chlorine from the compound so as not to harm the ozone layer, but they were extremely potent greenhouse gases themselves. The global warming potential (GWP)—the metric of how much heat a greenhouse gas traps in the atmosphere—of HFCs is, in fact, thousands of times higher than that of carbon dioxide. All of these compounds—CFCs, HFCs and hydrochlorofluorocarbons (HCFCs)—are collectively known as F-gases, the "F" standing for fluorine.

In the early 1990s, global warming was barely on the public radar, except for a few scientists, a few environmental NGOs and that eight-minute warning in Frank Capra's 1958 film for Bell Science Labs. But several scientists did sound the HFC global warming alarm, just as they had done for CFCs and the hole in the ozone.

Governments, regulators, chemical companies, manufacturers and the media ignored these early warning signals. However, in one of the first forays of big business into connecting environmental debt to serious financial consequences, the insurance industry joined this group of early messengers in the mid-1990s, when extreme weather started causing new patterns of flooding and natural disasters. In 1995, Frank Nutter, president of the Reinsurance Association of America, clearly stated: "The insurance industry is first in line to be affected by climate change. It could bankrupt the industry."[30]

Throughout the 1990s and 2000s, the chemical companies certainly knew the dangers and nevertheless proceeded to manufacture and sell HFCs as environmentally friendly. In 2007, I approached my cousin Sid Schlomann, one of the leaders of green building for the U.S. Postal Service, and asked him to consider air-conditioning methodologies that did not deploy HFCs. He sent me a link from the Honeywell website touting the environmentally friendly qualities of HFCs. According to the Intergovernmental Panel on Climate Change, in 2007, F-gases, the chemicals used in most refrigeration and cooling, were responsible for 17 percent of the world's global warming impact.[31] Not annual emissions but *impact*. These gases are incredibly dangerous, as the chemical companies certainly knew.

Greenpeace's Technology Breakthrough—GreenFreeze

The most surprising part of the HFC story is perhaps Greenpeace's role in developing an alternative technology and opening up global markets. This was a first for the organization, and it remains an extraordinary example of entrepreneurial campaigning.

In 1992, two Greenpeacers from Germany, Wolo Lohbeck and Harald Zindler, approached a group of inventors and engineers to come up with an alternative to HFCs. The engineers suggested that hydrocarbons with a GWP of 4 or less, instead of HFCs with a GWP of 2,000 or so, would work in domestic refrigerators as a coolant. Greenpeace then prototyped and tested this new type of HFC-free refrigerator and dubbed it GreenFreeze.[32]

But who would make these refrigerators and who would sell them? No one. Shortly thereafter, Wolo and Harald went to the public and somehow got 70,000 orders in three weeks (this is pre-Internet) by using the German equivalent of the Sears Catalog as well as a very creative public relations campaign. They then went back to the manufacturer that had built the prototype and asked, "Would you like to build a new refrigerator that has 70,000 pre-orders?" The answer, of course, was yes. In March 1993, the first GreenFreeze refrigerator rolled off the assembly line in the former East Germany. Since then, over 650 million HFC-free refrigerators have been sold around the world by leading manufacturers. Greenpeace open-sourced the technology and has taken no remuneration. (GreenFreeze refrigerators finally became legal in the United States on December 15, 2011, almost twenty years after they were introduced in Germany.)

Since the technology was introduced, manufacturers and retailers have taken over the business—as it should be. But Greenpeace has worked side by side with these companies in pushing government regulations, helping to open up markets, advocating for incentives for manufacturers, convening technology-sharing activities and introducing other non-HFC technologies to different industries.

Greenpeace Collaboration with Big Business—Coca-Cola

The single largest part of our value chain carbon footprint is our refrigeration equipment. We are a consumer goods company that depends on being loved in the marketplace every day. So in 2000, when Greenpeace asked us not so politely to eliminate HFCs, we listened and actually committed to find alternative ways of bringing cold beverages to our consumers. And we knew that we not only needed to replace climate-damaging F-gases, but also needed to meet and exceed current refrigeration efficiency performance if we were to really offer a better environmental solution. Today, our new cold drink equipment is the most energy efficient in the world, which is a huge advantage cost advantage for customers, and contributes to our continued leadership as the world's number one Brand. And we are helping innovate new non-HFC alternatives to change "business as usual" bring much needed climate solutions into the marketplace.

—Jeff Seabright, Vice President, Environment and
Water Resources, The Coca-Cola Company

Greenpeace gave Coca-Cola a migraine headache in 2000 by protesting its sponsorship of the so-called Green Olympics in Sydney, Australia, because of the company's decidedly not-green HFC coolers. Coke's polar bear icon was a perfect target. Greenpeace assembled protesters in polar bear costumes resembling the logo to "die" on cue at the entrance to the Olympics. This was not exactly the image desired by one of the world's top brands. Greenpeace asserted that eliminating HFCs was a better way to honor the polar bear.

Shortly thereafter, Greenpeace and Coca-Cola began talking, a conversation that has continued for over a dozen years. I was lucky enough to be at this table from 1995 to 2012. It was not always fun, but it always was constructive. I'm quite sure that the entire Coca-Cola team would agree that this collaborative work resides squarely in Coca-Cola's long-term self-interest. And Greenpeace staff has never failed to be impressed with the dedication, seriousness and creativity of the company's refrigeration team.

A team of exceptional people from Coca-Cola, including Jeff Seabright, Lisa Manley, Bryan Jacob, Salvatore Gabola, Steve Cousins and Antoine Azar, worked with Greenpeace on this issue. Over the course of the twelve-year collaboration, several Coca-Cola CEOs were also involved.

The company was moving forward but not fast enough for Greenpeace. In 2009, soon after Muhtar Kent became CEO, he made a bold decision: Coca-Cola would be the first company to eliminate HFCs from all new vending machines and cooling equipment by 2015. PERIOD. This was not business as usual; this was leadership.

Unilever

As early as 2000, it was clear that HFCs were serious contributors to global warming. It was equally clear that they would be regulated in the EU [European Union] at some point. Unilever is the largest ice cream company in the world, so we had to decide whether to move ahead of regulation or get caught in costly and difficult supply problems reacting to a new regulatory framework imposed upon us. The programme of work which our in-house engineers initiated with Greenpeace allowed us to take the leadership role in creating smart new technologies.

—Gavin Neath, former VP, Sustainability, Unilever

Unilever's Ben & Jerry's brand was the first to introduce an HFC-free commercial cooler into the U.S. market in 2009.[33] By that time, over 300,000 of Unilever's 2 million-plus fleet of ice cream dispensers and coolers had been deployed everywhere but North America. As solutions director of Greenpeace, I joined Alan Gerrard and Pete Gosselin of Unilever for the press conference announcing this North American debut. At dinner the night before, we learned that all the new technology had been developed by Alan and his team above and beyond their normal jobs—working as a group over countless nights and weekends, inspired by the company's 2000 commitment to eliminate HFCs. When Greenpeace USA research director Kert Davies and I asked Alan why he had done that, he responded that he loved his job, it supported him and his family well, but at the end of the day, "My job is keeping ice cream cold. If I go the extra mile and figure out how we can roll out HFC-free coolers, I have something I can tell my children I did for them that was long lasting and meaningful."

Alan and his team went beyond business as usual and designed the natural refrigeration technology for the company's ice cream coolers. Unilever is the largest ice cream company in the world (it includes Breyers, Heartbrand, Ben & Jerry's, Carte D'Or, Magnum, Popsicle, Klondike), so this was no small matter.

The company pursued its new technology with a vengeance. It introduced the first HFC-free coolers in Europe in 2003, and today Unilever has well over a million of these coolers deployed around the world. The natural refrigerant coolers are also more efficient than the HFC models, using about 15 percent less energy.

Alan Gerrard and his fellow engineers, with a special tip of the hat to Rene van Gerwen, exemplify the ingenuity and ambition we need to solve both business and environmental problems.

To illustrate the Unilever/Greenpeace relationship, three days before our joint 2009 U.S. press event, I received a call from a Greenpeace colleague that we were about to attack Unilever for its use of palm oil from Indonesia's threatened rain forests. I called Alan and offered to back out of the press conference. I didn't want to do anything to harm Unilever's good work on natural refrigerants, and I would never ask my colleagues to stop their action in Indonesia against the company. Alan called his senior management, who said we could go ahead with the joint press conference. I was obviously very relieved that Unilever agreed to a moratorium on Indonesian palm oil the next day. The company is now a global leader on responsible palm oil sourcing.

Refrigerants, Naturally!

Corporate collaboration that encourages economies of scale is one of the most important market mechanisms that can be deployed on behalf of the environment. Most environmental NGOs are always looking for this sweet spot. In 2004, Coca-Cola, Unilever and McDonald's created Refrigerants, Naturally! with Greenpeace and UNEP as founding supporters. The purpose was just as it sounds—to build a global initiative of companies committed to combating climate change by substituting natural refrigerants in place of harmful fluorinated gases.

PepsiCo

Pepsi joined Refrigerants, Naturally! in 2006 and also showed strong leadership in the group. Sustainability executives Cees-Jan Adema and David Walker, engineers Mike Saba and Emad Jafa and vice president Paul Boykas all helped push the refrigeration agenda inside and outside of the company. All played critical roles at different times and in different arenas to help move their industry away from these terrible chemicals. Cees-Jan Adema reached out to civil society organizations and political groups, and Mike Saba offered his expertise to competitors and other industries, including the auto industry.

One of my favorite anecdotes from a Refrigerants, Naturally! meeting occurred when an engineer from Pepsi asked an engineer from Coke, "Will you share this data with me?" Coke's engineer replied, "Of course, I share everything with you except for the formula for Coke." This putting aside of rivalry is exemplary.

Natural refrigerants just became legal in the United States in December 2011, nearly twenty years after they were introduced in Europe and about thirteen years after they were introduced Asia. In order to help change this, engineers from Coca-Cola, Pepsi and Unilever joined Greenpeace in briefing staff from three U.S. congressional subcommittees on Capitol Hill in 2009. You know the world is full of surprises when corporate engineers presented the science outlining the dangers of HFCs along with successful alternative technologies and Greenpeace advocated for incentives for the corporations. And we were all advocating for the inclusion of HFC regulation in the climate bill then being crafted, the

> Good ideas are not adopted automatically. They must be driven
> into practice with courageous impatience.
>
> —Admiral H. G. Rickover, U.S. Navy

Waxman-Markey Bill. And then, in 2010, the opportunity of a lifetime presented itself.

The Consumer Goods Forum

The Consumer Goods Forum (CGF), founded in June 2009, is a global network of over four hundred retailers, manufacturers, service providers and other stakeholders across seventy countries. Its member companies have combined sales of $3.5 trillion. Early on, the group decided to address sustainability. Refrigeration and cooling represents one of the top three pieces of many of their member companies' carbon footprint. Coca-Cola CEO Muhtar Kent was CGF's first co-chair.

After Muhtar committed Coca-Cola to eliminating HFCs in 2009, Greenpeace International executive director Kumi Naidoo asked him to persuade other corporations to also move to natural refrigerants. Muhtar responded beyond Kumi's most ambitious hopes by leading the transformation of the entire consumer goods sector. In addition to his environmental interest, he had the perfect motivation—the more companies that use natural refrigerant technologies, the lower the price from the supplier. This is how I ended up in that dull Chicago ballroom with a receptive audience to a request for radical change to change refrigeration technologies. This led to the CGF Refrigeration Resolution to eliminate HFCs from all new equipment starting in 2015.

Because the big CGF companies are leading the way to economies of scale, there will be a de facto dominant technology change soon after 2015. Since the CGF Resolution passed in 2010, retailers Sobey's of Canada, SuperValu of the United States, Aeon of Japan and Marks & Spencer of the United Kingdom are all shepherding a technology transformation that provides cheaper electricity bills and lower energy demand for the entire consumer goods sector while contributing to the fight against climate change. Not a bad payoff. But industry actions need a partner in government.

The EPA and the Regulatory Process

The EPA controls the licensing of new refrigeration technologies in the United States. For two decades, the EPA would not accept alternatives to HFCs because the agency claimed that natural refrigerants were flammable and dangerous. With several hundred million HFC-free refrigerators and cooling machines in use around the world, trillions of hours of safety and efficiency data were available. Even though the largest refrigerator manufacturers and suppliers in the world were selling safe, reliable equipment globally for almost two decades, these data never satisfied the EPA.

Because corporations did not want to antagonize the agency that regulated them, Greenpeace took the role of trying to push the EPA to change its regulations. The meetings were always difficult. I finally understood why corporations hate regulations. In several meetings over the seven years that I participated, it became clear that the EPA staff deferred to outdated regulations over the most current science.

Throughout the fight to legalize natural refrigerants in the United States, one division of the EPA used the Clean Air Act as a reason not to allow GreenFreeze-style hydrocarbon refrigerants to replace HFCs. Staff members claimed that the hydrocarbons would likely be vented, which was illegal under the CAA. Greenpeace calculated that if all the refrigerators in the United States were vented of hydrocarbons at the same time, it would have the same collective effect as 1,700 cans of paint. So, using

CAA as the reason, hydrocarbon refrigerators were deemed illegal by the EPA. The venting of these greener refrigerators would have a minuscule impact on air quality, and they would help prevent climate change. But the CAA was written before HFCs were invented or the term "climate change" appeared in the *Oxford English Dictionary*. That's the common sense that's missing from today's regulation.

Additionally, the EPA didn't consider the timeline and predictability a corporation needs in order to change its infrastructure, even for a good cause. One EPA staffer said, "We might even have a clear decision on natural refrigerants in nine months . . . but then again it might take several years." Obviously, no corporation could function on such a vague timeline when planning capital investment. I absolutely believe in tough environmental regulation, but I also believe that common sense belongs in the regulatory framework.

If government were mandated to incentivize good technology, the EPA would likely not have wasted twenty years in regulatory muck. The EPA's twenty years of stalling has allowed HFCs to become a huge industry that now has terrible real-world consequences. This is why the NMB Framework calls for strong government policy.

Conclusion

In the cases described in this chapter, corporate representatives of McDonald's, Tiffany, Walmart, Coca-Cola, PepsiCo and Unilever are demonstrating real courage in facing complicated and difficult environmental challenges. Many other corporate leaders are behaving similarly. However, these are only the first steps toward a business paradigm that coexists with nature. All of these companies still need to make huge changes in most aspects of their businesses. That is why the NMB Framework must become government policy—so corporate leaders are empowered to make large-scale changes on many more fronts.

The U.S. Congress can't get to square one in any climate legislation today, even though the science is more compelling than the pollution and health statistics of 1970. The Clean Air Act passed, against huge corporate objections, only because some incredibly brave politicians used their backbone along with all of their political, social and financial credit in pursuit of a greater common good. Senators Muskie and Baker proved themselves true public servants by risking their own political lives on behalf of their nation.

If we wish to maintain any clean air, land and water, not to mention sufficient food and shelter for the 7 billion souls on the planet, each of us must muster our own brand of courage—in the public, private and individual sectors.

> It is . . . nonsense to say that it does not matter which individual man acted as the nucleus for the change. It is precisely this that makes history unpredictable into the future.
>
> —Gregory Bateson, anthropologist, scientist, linguist

5

MOVING BEYOND FOSSIL FUELS

THE PUBLIC, PRIVATE AND INDIVIDUAL SECTORS

Electricity, automotive, air and sea transport are all necessary for our economy to survive, much less thrive. We must find energy sources to support them.

But fossil fuels, currently the primary source of this energy, endanger our very survival. They threaten not only our economy but our food and water supplies. It's that basic.

Only by understanding the full cost of our energy can we arrive at solutions to this exceptionally difficult and urgent set of problems.

Throughout this book, I have spoken of both the public and private sectors, with a serious nod to individual courage. But in the energy sector, more so than almost anywhere else, the individual is a truly distinct player—his or her own "sector." Renewable energy and efficiency will come to fruition only when you and I change many of our daily behaviors.

The good news is that a new cast of characters is shaking up the energy sector in both the public and private arenas, and young people are excited to claim better energy habits than their parents. I hope these young people will lead the individual sector as well.

While fossil fuel companies are duking it out for the unrestricted freedom to extract resources from Earth, there is a changing of the guard on the other end of the spectrum. The largest investments in the renewable sector are now coming from non-energy corporations, largely technology and information giants and Silicon Valley–style entrepreneurs. It appears that the energy industry is evolving from the extractive and centralized business it has been for the last century into a decentralized industry based on information technology (IT) and smart financial mechanisms. This new role for nonenergy business is big news.

And to confirm its importance to security, many of the world's largest military systems are aware that energy shortages can disrupt all economic and social systems. Whether on the battlefield or in the computer systems that govern and facilitate financial markets, or in the logistics operations that deliver food and water, energy is central to our functional lives.[1]

NO ENERGY SECURITY, NO NATIONAL SECURITY

As we saw earlier, Google has invested over $1 billion in renewable energy and made a commitment to carbon neutrality in 2007. Google's investments secure its own huge data center energy needs and also advance the grid for regional utilities, like the company's 2012 wind power project in Oklahoma and 2010 mid-Atlantic wind offshore grid investment.[2] Facebook, Microsoft, Samsung, IBM and other technology companies are also ramping up their investments in renewable energy, including working with energy-neutral contractors and builders.[3]

Many companies, such as Cisco, are investing in product development to rein in unmanaged energy costs. Cisco estimates that its EnergyWise protocol can actually eliminate 20 percent of energy usage and costs.[4] EnergyWise is an intelligent energy management solution that monitors, controls and reports the energy use of a building's or company's IT and facilities equipment.

Satisfying the world's energy demands is complicated and demands that we look at more complicated data than the current price per kilowatt-hour (kWh) of electricity or gallon of gasoline. Those prices are mere contributors to an economy that is racking up huge environmental debt. The debt is now due, and it must be incorporated into the price we pay for energy.

It's Really Complex

When I was growing up, the totality of my understanding of electricity came from my smooth ability to turn lights on and off and some really good movies about coal miners. I did also live through a few intense New York City blackouts, so I understood that there was a serious problem if the lights went off. That was before computers governed and guided almost every aspect of our daily existence. Today, virtually everything requires electricity, including the telephone system, which, for some reason, cable companies are now hooking up to computer routers. I find this so disturbing because if the lights go out, so does the landline telephone. Also, one has to keep a whole system on (I turn off all routers and cable systems at night and when computers are off) in order to power something that worked perfectly fine without electricity previously.

I don't have a car in New York City. I do take a taxi pretty regularly and use cars when I'm anywhere outside of a big city. But I take airplanes a lot—for both work and pleasure.

A Greenpeace buddy returned from a San Francisco Exploratorium exhibit where visitors measured their carbon footprint. He explained how he was ticking away at the boxes, feeling good about himself—mass transit, check; recycle and reuse stuff, check; overall consumption, check—and then he got to air travel. He was shocked to learn the extent of the impact of his global air travel. It canceled out all the good of his other consumption patterns. I'm in the same boat.

In the 1980s, I delved into the dangers of nuclear and coal energy a bit as a volunteer and board member for Greenpeace, and I also served as a political appointee on the Transportation Advisory Committee for Greater Seattle. But most of what I know about electricity and transportation I learned in the last fifteen years, when I started reading about global warming—now more accurately called climate change. Fossil fuel energy and climate change are inextricably linked, so I've had to bone up on the solutions to the problem: renewables and efficiency. And after fifteen years, the complexity of the finances, technology and resources around energy continues to confound, not least because they're in a constant state of flux.

When I started writing this book over a year ago, the race for oil in the Arctic had only just begun. (How ironic that the loss of sea ice caused by climate change allows the same companies that largely deny the phenomenon entirely to drill for more oil.) Two years ago, huge natural gas reserves had not yet been discovered, wind energy was booming (now it is in a serious slump) and solar energy cost about double what it does today.

Fossil fuel companies spend so much money on advertising, lobbying and disinformation that real data are intentionally obfuscated. Despite the industry's well-funded climate change denial campaign, science unequivocally states that fossil fuels, through both extraction and combustion, are primarily responsible for climate change—the largest piece of our environmental debt.

I am sure that some of this chapter will be out of date by the time you are reading it. However, the companion website to chapter 8, "A Transition Agenda," will be updated continually with both progress and obstacles. In the virtual and real forums, solutions and alternatives will be thoroughly deliberated—mostly by other experts, but with crowdsourcing leadership to incorporate your ideas and actions. I hope that by the end of this chapter, you will have a radically changed understanding of what is expensive and what is dangerous in the field of energy. Our energy choices are rarely what they seem.

> And if all others accepted the lie which the Party imposed—if all records told the same tale—then the lie passed into history and became truth.
>
> —George Orwell, *1984*

I've divided this chapter into two parts. The first focuses on renewable energy, as it pertains to the true cost and replacement value of coal. The second part is about transportation and oil.

Liberating our economy from fossil fuels is the most urgent need of our times—both for our environment and for our financial well-being.

Renewable Energy

The photo on the next page shows a sticker on the back window of a miner's car at Arch Coal's Raven coal-preparation plant in Knott County, Kentucky. It's how most miners feel about the product they produce to power the country.[5]

There are things that the Friends of Coal are not telling you.

I could recite hundreds, maybe thousands, of statistics to tell this story. Instead, I want to tell the story of the real costs and

Photograph by Bill Estes / Lexington Herald-Leader.

real benefits of how we spend our energy dollars. I am omitting any discussion of nuclear power because I believe it will die of its own accord. It's too expensive, with very few private financing options, and very few governments will continue to invest in or guarantee new construction . . . except Iran or other governments especially interested in using the nuclear fuel as a cover for weapons programs. China is investing in nuclear plants because it is investing heavily in every kind of energy system. In several other countries where plant construction or licensing has begun, new plants will likely continue to completion, but the technology remains troublesome and more costly in the long term than renewable alternatives. And as we know, when there is a nuclear problem, it's a whopper.[6] Also, finding a safe repository for spent fuel has proven elusive, expensive and intractable. In my opinion, nuclear energy is a nonstarter.

Energy is an issue that is simultaneously public and private. We as individuals are central players in lowering energy demand, whether it involves weatherizing our buildings (homes, offices or public institutions); using energy-monitoring devices on our appliances; lowering heat or air conditioning use; or driving fewer miles in smaller vehicles, biking, walking and taking mass transit.

I have been waiting for an American president to ask the country to lower our energy use by 20 percent within a year. That's what Japan did in the wake of the Fukushima disaster. I hope that in Transition Agenda forums, with strong leadership from everyday citizens—Parents for Climate Change Protection, student governments of all ages, parent-teacher associations, reading clubs and bowling leagues—we can recapture the excitement of achieving what feels impossible. The individual sector *can* eliminate every bit of wasted and unnecessary energy. A Transition Agenda will offer expertise and advice. You will provide the leadership and action.

One of renewable energy's biggest advantages, as an industry of the future, is its large reliance on decentralized operations, installation and distribution. But this model also makes renewables and efficiency more complicated to ramp up than building a new Hoover Dam or a big nuclear power plant. Decentralized energy means that many players, many financiers and many regulations must align before taking action. In contrast, large centralized power plants are organized and financed by a few big corporations, corporate or government bonds, a few big contractors (i.e., Bechtel or Halliburton) along with some government oversight and regulations. The same players have been running the game for decades.

Danny Kennedy, founder of Sungevity, a booming solar company in California, told the *New York Times* recently, "Think about it this way. We're killing people in foreign lands in order to extract 200-million-year-old sunlight. Then we burn it . . . in order to boil water to create steam to drive a turbine to generate electricity. We frack our own backyards and pollute our rivers, or we blow up our mountaintops just miles from our nation's capital for an hour of electricity, when we could just take what's falling free from the sky."[7]

While I wholeheartedly agree with Danny's sentiment, that last part is not entirely true. Cheap energy sounds very appealing, but at the moment it does not exist. Happily, a handful of pioneers in technology, business and policy have finally demonstrated enough success in bringing renewable energy to scale that a path forward is emerging. If we can build a strong infrastructure (including a smart grid and new storage capacity technology), these "free" fuels (wind, sun, geothermal, wave) may become quite cheap in the future. But don't let anyone tell you that *getting there* will be cheap. It will not.

In addition to getting our heads around a new service model, we'll have to fight some very entrenched interests in the move to renewables. The fossil fuel industry has made big companies and powerful nations very rich. It also powers much of the world's financial engine. Yet the difficulty of the task only underlines its crucial importance.

> When it is obvious that the goals cannot be reached, don't adjust the goals, adjust the action steps.
>
> —Confucius

A Renewable Energy Economy Is Attainable Sooner Than You Think

A big piece of this story, like any other, is the money. Always follow the money.

Right now, wind and solar are very small pieces of the energy mix in the United States, but they are growing rapidly. However, in other parts of the world, renewables are already major players.

Europe's strong renewable policies have created a revolution in energy sourcing. Germany produced a record-breaking amount of solar electricity in September 2012—the equivalent of twenty large nuclear power stations.[8] And in the European Union during the same period, wind provided the equivalent of thirty-nine midsize nuclear plants or a train of coal stretching from Buenos Aires to Brussels.[9]

When good policy—price supports and subsidies—launches an industry, the industry takes off, and prices come down. Presuming a good product, the market then takes over. Today, China's massive solar and wind subsidies are artificially confusing prices, supply and demand throughout the world, and these technology markets are momentarily crashing as a result. But these subsidies have helped launch the installation and employment side of this industry. In fact, in early 2013 labor unions in Europe fought against tariffs on these cheap Chinese imports. If the rest of the world's governments decided to move with similar urgency to ramp up these industries, the market would look quite different.

For customers in the United States, the best buy in electricity today comes via the California Solar Initiative (CSI). Created in response to Governor Arnold Schwarzenegger's call, in 2004, for the creation of 1 million solar roofs in the California, it has transformed the state's energy market. In this installation plan, a building owner pays nothing up front, commits to a ten-year energy buy (at lower prices than current ones) and has solar installed on the building for free. The new system is transferable to the building's next owners, and the cost is included in all mortgage transactions. This is a great deal that cost California only $3 billion over ten years.[10] The plan sunsets in 2016. CSI offers three big benefits: It eliminates greenhouse gas emissions, satisfies peak demand needs (which allows utilities to *not* build expensive new power plants) and helps mainstream installation know-how as well as the technology itself. Peak demand is the daily spike in energy usage when temperatures are highest (or coldest); businesses have the most computers and other electronics running; and all public buildings have high concentrations of elevators, machines and other energy systems in use.

The financing mechanism of the CSI installation effort was created by Jigar Shah, founder of SunEdison, one of the world's leading solar services company. The SunEdison business model, whereby building owners do not own equipment but instead lease electricity, remains an important innovation that helped turn solar into a multibillion-dollar industry worldwide.

The solar industry is one of the fastest-growing industries in the United States.[11] In 2011, it employed 100,000 people, 26,000 of them in California.[12] Most of these people sell, install and service whole systems. Currently, the industry is doubling in size every four years, but with good policy incentives, it could move much faster, becoming both an employment and an energy engine.

The cost of solar in California has gone from up to 36 cents to 7 cents/kWh since CSI's inception.[13] And in 2008, a new cost-neutral federal funding mechanism, Property Assessed Clean Energy (PACE), came onto the market. PACE finances energy efficiency and renewable upgrades to buildings by offering building owners full financing, repaid as a property tax assessment for up to twenty years.[14] These upgrades increase the value of the buildings and save money on energy costs. As of 2012, twenty-eight states are participating. Essentially, PACE is mimicking the CSI funding mechanism, but without the cost to taxpayers. This is how government can successfully vitalize a new technology that benefits everyone. It launches smart long-term policy with adequate funding and regulations, and the objective becomes viable and competitive in the commercial market.

Although solar panel manufacturing has some emissions, solar plants have none.[15]

Solar plant in California—no emissions.

Compare some of the costs and savings. CSI plans to generate 1,940 megawatts (MW) of solar energy by 2016 with a budget of $3 billion. This amount approximates what utility Duke Energy spent on each of its most recent coal-fired plants in Indiana and North Carolina. Both coal plants generate less electricity than CSI.[16]

So when you hear people say that renewables cannot possibly meet our energy demand, ask a lot of questions. And presume you have to be part of the solution.

> An ounce of prevention is worth a pound of cure.
>
> —Benjamin Franklin

The best money energy activists can spend is on lowering demand. The sheer expense of meeting peak demand underlines how important our personal actions are. Downloading a movie or using the dishwasher or washing machine during off-peak hours instead of at high noon or eliminating standby usage can seriously lower energy demand.

Most electronics suck small amounts of energy even when they are in the off position, unless they are fully turned off by a surge protector or unplugged. This wasted energy is called vampire or standby power. Because so many of us use so many electronic devices—televisions, sound systems, computers, routers, printers, personal digital assistants—these tiny bits of electricity usage add up. Vampire electricity currently accounts for between 5 and 10 percent of all power usage in the United States.[17] Since satisfying peak demand is probably the costliest part of the electricity puzzle, a few surge protectors and big changes in individual habits could alter the energy cost/benefit analysis.

Here's the choice. Would you rather turn off your computer/game/electronics systems overnight and when no one is home all day or pay for the building of a new power plant to accommodate peak demand? I have asked friends to do this, and several have answered, "But it takes so long for the computer to reboot." Isn't this two-minute wait a small price to pay for being part of the global energy solution?

On the subject of efficiency, I must share a family tiff caused by my own tactlessness. I was visiting my brilliant cousin, whom I adore, and he was washing the dishes after a delicious dinner. Unfortunately, he kept running the hot water while talking to me and slowly going about his work. I'm sure I was brusque and pushy when I mentioned it was not a good idea to keep the hot water running; he got very upset. But the point remains: The way most of us wash dishes uses extra water and energy for no good reason. Changing this one habit is not enough to lower peak demand on energy plants, but it is one of the dozens of reflexive habits most of us have when it comes to energy. If most of us changed many of these behaviors, the sum total of our individual actions could actually contribute to a decrease in energy demand.

We have to begin viewing our individual actions as the individual sector of energy efficiency. We are a renewable energy resource.

Wind power is also becoming a significant source of energy, getting cheaper because of government subsidies due to end in 2013. In 2012, wind power supplied 3.25 percent of all electricity in the United States. While the technology has been supported by government contracts and corporate research and design for many years, it faces continual threats of the subsidies being cut off. Although this constant uncertainty has been a nightmare for the market, wind power has continued to grow, and its price has continued to decrease—until 2012. Overcapacity, lack of government support and short-term financial concerns are limiting investment in new wind globally in 2013. But the U.S. Department of Energy predicts in its Levelized Cost of Energy chart, shown in the appendix to this chapter, that wind is expected to be cheaper than coal, nuclear, solar and virtually every other power source besides natural gas in 2017.[18]

In New York City, where I have opted for electricity generated by wind power, it costs me almost double what Con Edison charges for juice (mostly from hydro and natural gas). I get upset every month when I receive my bill.

But in Illinois, where hundreds of communities are aggregating their energy purchases, wind power is already cheaper than conventional energy sources. This is small potatoes now, but the former director of the Illinois Power Authority notes that aggregation could prove to be "the largest economic development project in the state."[19]

The mid-Atlantic–Midwest utility PJM Interconnection (which has 60 million customers) has used a combination of efficiency, demand response (encouraging reduced use during peak times) and renewables to move away from some big dirty coal plants. Using efficiency in its dispatch mechanisms to manage peak load, the company saved nearly $200 million in 2011 and has accumulated savings of $455 million since 2008. This is different from the efficiencies you and I might deploy in our homes or other buildings—and, boy, did it work. PJM's savings were virtually equal to its operating costs! The company notes: "Combustion turbines, gas or oil-fired generators that use air combustion to produce power, are often on-stand-by to run if needed because they can be brought on-line more quickly. However, the cost of having them available and running them are typically more expensive than previously scheduled generation."[20] This, again, shows the high cost of satisfying peak demand.

And PJM now has enough solar capacity to power 1.5 percent of its customer base, nearly 1 million homes.

The State of Texas has the most wind power of any state— wind power accounted for 6.9 percent of the electricity generated there in 2011.[21] Many cities and states use wind to power their government-owned buildings. But in Texas, companies like Kohl's, Whole Foods and Hilton Hotels, which have larger buying profiles than most city administrations, use solar and wind for most or all of their power needs.[22]

In every possible scenario, public, private and individual sectors will spend trillions of dollars on energy in a variety of forms over the next decade. The choice is *where* to spend the money, not *whether* to spend it. And the only sensible move is to focus on safe and secure renewables and efficiency. Some will argue that governments can't afford the kind of subsidies needed to make it work, yet a review of the external costs shows indisputably that we are already incurring huge environmental debt. This is what the politicians still won't say, even as many businesses start speaking the language of long-term and external costs.

Externalities: The New Math for
Public and Private Investment

The true cost of coal is between 18 and 27 cents per kWh, not the 8 cents you see on your utility bill.

The true cost of gasoline is about $13 per gallon (in the United States), not the $4 to $5 (or less) we pay at the pump.

The combined external costs of just coal and oil from one year equal the entire annual federal deficit in the United States—about $1.3 trillion.

The cheap energy that fuels the American economy isn't free. It all incurs environmental debt, much of which contributes to the federal deficit. As I write today in October 2012, Hurricane Sandy has shut down the East Coast of the United States at enormous cost. This storm was so intense because of extra-warm ocean waters that have altered the normal course of the jet stream. Normal ocean currents would have pushed much of this storm out to sea. The storm is a direct collision of financial and environmental debt.

In 2011, in a peer-reviewed report, Harvard's Institute for Global Health and the Environment concluded that just in the United States, coal's external costs—including environmental cleanup and treatment of related health problems—total between $350 and $500 billion every year. Imagine if your electric bill tripled, as did the embedded electric costs of everything you bought. We are already paying these costs; we just don't realize it because they don't show up on our monthly statements.

We pay for these costs in taxes. Federal, state and city budgets cover these costs through expenses for hospitals, schools, water and waste systems and emergency services. Private businesses cover these costs through expensive water treatment and insurance reimbursements for death, health benefits and property loss. Individual families cover these costs through everything from health care to taxes.

This is a bad way to make energy policy. All public money is not equal.

Taxes that support a young person's education or the infrastructure that creates high-speed Internet are investments that keep on giving for a generation or two. Taxes that support the cleanup of coal or oil spills, increased instances of cancer or mental retardation or fighting more frequent and intense wildfires all incur a negative return on investment for the public coffers. We have to view our public energy investments with this fuller picture in mind.

According to the prevailing wisdom, we cannot afford to move to renewable energy because it will bankrupt the economy. This is a ruse.

Former South Carolina congressional conservative Republican Bob Inglis says:

> If you correct the market distortions and make all fuels accountable for all of their costs, that will drive innovation, and as a result reduce CO_2 emissions. The freebies for coal and petroleum are substantial even if you leave out the climate change impacts—just consider the health impacts, or attach to petroleum some of the defense costs in the Persian Gulf. We want the accountability that is a key value of social-issue conservatives, who believe, as I do, that human beings are responsible actors. The argument to social-issue conservatives will be, if you're coal, you gotta be accountable! If you're causing 23,600 premature deaths in the U.S. annually, over 3 million lost work days annually, pay up![23]

Congressman Inglis obviously believes that pollution can no longer be free, and I'm sorry to report that he lost his seat in 2010 in part due to this belief. If only his constituents understood the math! That's one of the big reasons I have written this book. The real math has to enter all public and private policy debates on energy. "A Transition Agenda" (chapter 8) shows where and how you can help change the conversation.

Mike Carr, the former Democratic senior counsel of the U.S. Senate Energy Committee, speaking publicly but *as an individual*, said, "The mother of all subsidies in the energy game is not pricing in the externalities and imposing them on the rest of society."[24] As an Energy Committee staffer, he oughta know.

There are calls from every sector to account for climate change risk in financial reporting. This includes do-good groups like Conservation International; insurance companies like Munich Re; government agencies like Maryland's State Treasury and the U.S. government's Securities and Exchange Commission; financial sector groups like the Investors Network for Climate Risk ($10 trillion in assets) and the Global Reporting Initiative; dozens of multinational corporations; and many international militaries. All of these groups experience the effects of climate change in different ways, and all express the need to ramp up alternatives to fossil fuel. In fact, the U.S. military is one of the largest developers of fossil fuel alternatives for both energy and transport.[25]

The public rarely recognizes externalities until an oil rig blows up in the Gulf of Mexico or a nuclear plant melts down on the coast of Japan, or when hurricanes, tornadoes and typhoons become more intense globally. But, in fact, the costs of traditional energy sources are felt everywhere, and by everyone, in more quotidian ways. Water, land and air are always under attack when it comes to fossil fuel use.

The value of our money is not as simple as a cheap price for energy as noted on our bill. This is the real math, and these are the real choices. With real information, you be the judge of the smartest use of our money.

Jobs

Coal industry sheds jobs, leaving Eastern Kentucky economy in tatters.
—*Lexington Herald-Leader,* July 29, 2012

As this newspaper headline notes, coal jobs are disappearing, largely due to competition from cheaper and cleaner natural gas. A year ago, wind power employed more people than coal mining in the United States. As of September 2012, the wind industry is in a free fall, and very little new capacity is anticipated for 2013 due to lack of government support and an oversupply of turbines and other products.[26] Yet wind (and solar) still employs more people than coal. And as we saw before, a new cast of characters is bringing both jobs and renewable energy to the market.

The electronics company Samsung has already invested billions of dollars in renewable energy in Australia and is now investing another $7 billion to build 2,500 MW of wind and solar farms in Ontario—the largest cluster of wind and solar on the planet. Samsung credits good Ontario policy with the move: "Thanks to Samsung's Green Energy Investment Agreement with the Government of Ontario, we will create 16,000 jobs, kick-start a new industry in Ontario and generate 2,500 megawatts of clean energy—enough to power 600,000 Ontario homes. This is all thanks to some of the most ambitious legislation in North America, which has sent a powerful message to the world that Ontario is open for business and to new jobs and investment."[27]

That is exactly why Ontario passed its Green Energy Act in 2009. The official website of the province states: "Ontario's Green Energy Act was created to expand renewable energy generation, encourage energy conservation and promote the creation of clean [16,000] energy jobs."[28]

In Japan, government spending on feed-in tariffs (price supports) has also spurred the solar and wind industries. The output from renewables in September 2012 is comparable to that of a large nuclear reactor. Post-Fukushima, those feed-in tariffs feel like an especially smart expenditure.[29]

These investments, and California's CSI, show government energy policy and funding working as it should.

Anything I write today may be different by the time you read this book. But one thing's for sure: The need for good jobs is not going away anytime soon. How about creating jobs that solve large energy problems and large environmental ones? Those might even be jobs less vulnerable to the vicissitudes of a crazy market—once that market incorporates true costs and benefits into its pricing.

In Kentucky, where coal is king, a local agency, Mountain Area Community Economic Development (MACED), calculated that the State of Kentucky provided a net subsidy of $115 million to the coal industry in 2006. MACED added the costs of transport on roads; costs of regulating environmental, health and safety; coal worker training; R&D for the coal industry; and a few other off-budget items. It did not include the external costs of water treatment or infrastructure, lost productivity resulting from injury and health impacts and the social and health costs of

The Impact of Coal on the Kentucky State Budget
Fiscal Year 2006

Revenues	
Industry-generated	$303,172,748
Generated from direct employment	$83,040,392
Generated from indirect employment	$141,509,362
Total Revenues	**$527,722,502**

Tax Expenditures (Foregone Revenues)	
Off-budget items (tax expenditures) specific to coal	(84,753,280)

On-budget Expenditures	
On-budget items supporting coal	(270,467,828)
Support for direct employment	(73,140,605)
Support for indirect employment	(214,192,262)
Total Expenditures	**($642,553,975)**
Net Impact	**($114,831,474)**

Source: Mountain Association for Community Economic Development

poor air quality. So, even among a constituency for whom coal is both lifeline and livelihood, the value of coal might be overrated. In reality, it might cause undue financial, medical and environmental burdens. MACED's chart shows the net impact of coal in Kentucky.

Consider the long-term value of allocating public and private funds to retrain coal workers, overhaul the coal industry, build a renewable grid, weatherize all American buildings and create a secure energy future that does not rely on coal. Now compare that to the long-term value of continuing to subsidize the coal industry as it exists today. All of us want cheap energy—but that ship has sailed. And the transition to more expensive energy will not be seamless.

Efficiency and renewable energy are the foundations of a vibrant employment program with huge long-term benefits for everyone, if we have the courage to embrace the change.

Petroleum and Transportation

The discovery of oil launched a revolution in the twentieth century. Travel changed radically, and newfangled materials made of petroleum transformed daily life. I recognize the privilege of growing up in the era where petroleum allowed me to get around easily in automobiles (especially convertibles), see the world via jet airplanes, listen to recorded music and use disposable diapers, take-out food containers and credit cards. Not to mention the tremendous convenience from synthetic fibers and rubber, medical and hygiene advances, packaging, paint, refrigerators and hundreds of other applications, including all the electronics and communication devices we use for work and pleasure every day.

To make matters even more complicated, oil holds the world hostage as a foreign policy lever. As futurist Gerald Celente famously asked, "You think we'd be in Iraq if the major export there was broccoli?"[30] Oil demands a huge amount of blood and treasure from all who touch it, use it and profit from it.

And now that climate change has caused the summer sea ice to melt in the Arctic, many of those same companies and countries want to risk even more for the chance at some new pots of money. But other oil companies view the risk as too great. Christophe de Margerie, chief executive of French oil multinational Total, told the *Financial Times* that the risk of an oil spill in such an environmentally sensitive area as the Arctic was simply too high. "Oil on Greenland would be a disaster," he said. "A leak would do too much damage to the image of the company."[31]

I saw *The Green Table Ballet* as a child (and many times since). Even at age ten, its clear representation of power (the human kind) hit me in the gut. The ballet, first performed in 1932, tells the story of gentlemen planning for war and then divvying up the spoils after the carnage. Today the oil companies and nations looking to the Arctic as the next frontier are on footing that will almost certainly lead to a resource war of terrible consequence.

Gentlemen in Black—The Green Table Ballet.

Photo by John Ross

But moving away from cars and oil will be extraordinarily difficult. In the United States especially, our land use, zoning, housing and employment centers are all based on the automobile. There are harbingers of good news, but to be honest, they are few and far between.

Between 1988 and 1991, I was a member of the Citizens Transportation Advisory Committee in Seattle. Our role was to oversee public spending on transportation in the tri-county region. It was a depressing exercise. The moment to build serious mass transit was upon us, but for a variety of not-very-good excuses, mostly about money, the region lost the opportunity.

At the time, the three counties around Seattle were booming in population, housing and roads. The big increase in employment was in the suburbs (think Microsoft in Redmond and Costco in Kirkland). And the highways that were empty when I arrived in Seattle in 1981 were becoming seriously crowded ten years later. Today, Greater Seattle's traffic problem is the seventh worst in the United States. And the greenbelt that once encircled the city has been replaced with strip malls, megamalls and low-density housing. Although there are some new Northwest train lines and a few more coming on line, along with ferries and vanpools and new high-occupancy vehicle lanes, the area's current investment (time, money and courage) in transportation is nowhere near the scale needed to address the problem.

Externalities of Oil

The United States currently boasts the cheapest gas prices in the world, and it has historically been the largest contributor to the planet's dangerous greenhouse gas load. China is now the largest emitter and is also catching up in terms of car ownership and energy usage (although per capita, China remains way behind the United States). If gas were to cost its real price per gallon at the pump, the entire U.S. economy would go into shock. The next chart shows that the rest of the world is already paying a more realistic price per gallon. This price is an exceedingly vulnerable piece of the American economic structure.

Premium Gasoline
Price Per Gallon July 2012 ($USD)

RANK

Country	Rank	Price
Norway	1	$10.12
Israel	3	$9.28
Hong Kong	4	$8.61
Netherlands	5	$8.26
Sweden	8	$8.14
UK	10	$7.87
France	11	$7.79
Germany	13	$7.74
Japan	18	$7.15
South Korea	19	$7.12
Brazil	21	$6.92
New Zealand	25	$6.55
Argentina	39	$5.82
Canada	40	$5.46
India	43	$5.44
China	45	$4.89
Russia	49	$3.75
USA	49	$3.75
Iran	54	$2.80
Saudi Arabia	59	$0.61
Venezuela	60	$0.09

Sources: Bloomberg, Gas Buddy and Wikipedia

Lester Brown, the founder of Worldwatch Institute and founder and president of the Earth Policy Institute, explained gas prices to the *Huffington Post*. The total of oil's "indirect costs centers around $9 per gallon, somewhat higher than the social cost of smoking a pack of cigarettes. Add this external or social cost to the roughly $2 per gallon average price of gasoline in the United States in early 2005, and gas would cost $11 a gallon (this does not include projected costs of climate change). These costs are real; someone bears them."[32]

On the opposite end of the political spectrum, the late Milton Copulus concurred with Mr. Brown. Copulus was head of the National Defense Council Foundation, former principal energy analyst for the Heritage Foundation, twelve-year member of the National Petroleum Council, Reagan White House alum and advisor to half a dozen U.S. Energy Secretaries, various secretaries of defense and two directors of the Central Intelligence Agency. In other words, he had serious conservative cred.

In 2006, Copulus measured the hidden cost of oil in the United States at $825.1 billion per year (not including climate change), adding $8.35 to the price of a gallon of gasoline refined from Persian Gulf oil, which would make the cost of filling a sedan a staggering $220 and an SUV, $325. Oil's environmental debt is incredibly hard to quantify and it is almost incomprehensible.[33]

And that debt is now coming due, both environmentally and financially.

Yesterday I was walking in the SoHo neighborhood of lower Manhattan at 5 P.M. while commuters were idling in traffic, honking their horns, waiting to enter the Holland Tunnel to New Jersey. My first thought was: The air is disgusting, I can barely breathe. My next thought was: This makes no sense. It is cheaper and faster to take public transit from most places in New Jersey to New York City than to drive. These cars, mostly driven by single commuters, easily had a forty-five-minute wait to go the ten blocks to get into the tunnel. Then they had all the traffic in the tunnel and on the other side. That's several hours of traffic misery. No one in this daily traffic jam would be home in less than an hour and a quarter. Yet the same scene can be seen any other day.

It's the epitome of bad financial and time management. The cost to use the tunnel during peak times is $9.50 round trip, and monthly parking in Manhattan ranges from $375 to $750. In comparison, the monthly pass on NJ Transit from Short Hills, New Jersey, to Penn Station (Manhattan) is $233. If commuters then need to take a subway or bus in Manhattan, it's an additional $104 for a monthly pass. This means that the public transit ride is less than the cost of the parking alone in Manhattan. Annual cost of public transit is $4,044 versus automobile commuting weighing in at approximately $15,000 per person (including parking, tolls, gas and cost of the car). The public commute is cheaper, *way* shorter and you can text!

Obviously some people need to drive, and in many American cities, there is no fast and convenient public transportation choice. But even where there is, so many eschew it for the comfort of an automobile that it suggests an intractable social behavior.

Yet automobile pollution has a near-term externality that everyone can understand. People who live near places with intense car or bus congestion suffer extremely high asthma and respiratory disease rates. The drivers are not paying these health costs or suffering these illnesses. As a taxpayer, I would rather pay for good mass transit and a more expensive nonpolluting bus than emergency room visits and dozens of other costs caused by fossil fuel combustion. Mass transit can be as cheap as vanpools or as expensive as high-speed rail or as preemptive as smart zoning and good bicycle infrastructure.

Government's role in creating good transportation infrastructure cannot be overemphasized, since it will most likely never be the jurisdiction of private industry.

In the New York metro area, which has the nation's highest transit ridership, whenever NJTransit brings on new lines and new trains, they are operating at capacity within months. Six months after the East River ferry started offering boats to connect Manhattan and Brooklyn, ridership was four times what had been projected. Imagine if these transit improvements became a real government priority, so that even people who are not inclined to take public transit could not resist the fast, convenient and cheap way to travel.

To accomplish this, all public transit would have to become more frequent and comfortable. Waiting for a bus or train, not knowing when it's coming and not having a rain shelter or a place to sit can be infuriating. I recently had the experience of waiting for a bus in Manhattan for forty-five minutes. When I called dispatch (I'm pushy, I got through), I was told that it could not identify where the specific buses were and that one should be coming any minute. Dispatch couldn't identify a bus location! That is a sorry tale in 2012, when even I know that GPS could do this simple task.

If more of us start using our local public transportation systems (even occasionally), increased ridership would help convince elected officials to spend more to improve the system. Especially if more of us simultaneously advocated strongly for this change in national priorities. For me, mass transit is often more pleasant, faster and less stressful than driving and parking your own car. Not always though.

For the times when only a car will do, the most promising alternative to petroleum is natural gas synthesized from sewage and animal waste. This nonextractive natural gas flows directly into the same natural gas pipelines that carry the conventional stuff that people are fighting about every day. In the European Union, new research and development money is spurring development of this nascent technology. Biomethane natural gas for transport eliminates and utilizes methane pollution from agricultural waste. By using waste, it does not compete with food production. I wish I could report that it's a booming industry, but it remains miniscule and is only now receiving some serious government investment. New natural gas discoveries make biomethane natural gas a very hard sell.

Sweden, Poland and the United Kingdom are all pioneering this potentially valuable and high-impact fuel, and Los Angeles County is just beginning to deploy a biogas fleet of buses. The U.S. Navy was experimenting with gas from waste to power ships, vehicles and planes in 2012. In the name of deficit reduction, U.S. congressmen attacked the U.S. military for spending $27 per gallon for the fuel versus the $3.50 per gallon for regular gasoline. That's because environmental debt has not yet entered the public discourse when debating federal spending. This budget equation must soon include full-cost variables.

Also, remember that solar energy cost up to 36 cents per kWh in 2009, and in 2012 it cost about 8 cents per kWh. New technologies that serve many masters are urgently needed, and I hope that biogas as a replacement fuel for oil grows in accessibility in both price and availability.

The individual sector's participation in biking and walking is also hugely important. Cities are responding to increased bike use by commuters and developing accordingly. The moment good and expanded bike lanes are put into place, a significant number of individuals choose to bike as an actual commuting choice. In Italy last year, more bicycles were sold than cars for the first time since World War II. Of course, the country is in financial free-fall, and I am not advocating following anything about the Italian economic system. However, when 10 percent of Italy's 60 million people bike to work, the long-beloved Italian culture may have something new and unexpected to offer.[34]

In the United States, surprising cities top the bike-commuting list. Most seem like they would be hard places to ride, but they

U.S. Bicycle Commuting Growth, 2000-2011

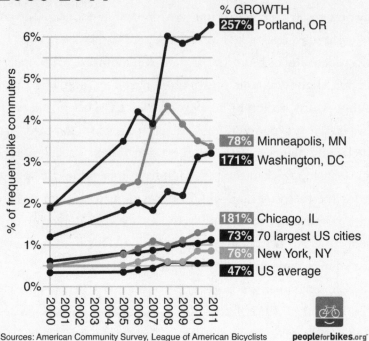

% GROWTH
257% Portland, OR

78% Minneapolis, MN
171% Washington, DC

181% Chicago, IL
73% 70 largest US cities
76% New York, NY
47% US average

Sources: American Community Survey, League of American Bicyclists   **peopleforbikes.org**

also share a culture that fosters a healthy lifestyle and an active commute. In rainy Portland, Oregon, 6 percent of workers ride to work on a regular basis. In snowy Minneapolis, 4 percent, and in hilly Seattle and San Francisco, 3 percent each. Smaller cities are not included in this ranking, but Boulder, Colorado, and Eugene, Oregon, have higher bike-commuting rates than Portland does.[35]

If we are to break our oil addiction, the public, private and individual sectors all need a transportation revolution.

Perhaps most problematically, we are accustomed to buying things more cheaply than other countries—especially gasoline. And our public transportation infrastructure lags behind that of most of the rest of the industrialized world. Subways in Bangkok,

Cairo and Delhi outshine most of America's. For some reason I honestly don't get, Americans object to paying for good public transit systems. The car culture is more entrenched in the United States than anywhere else in the world.

Alternative cars and fuels are coming to market. The two most promising areas are biogas (mentioned earlier) and switchable battery electric vehicles (explained in chapter 6). Both of these industries are still in their infancy, and despite serious efforts, I was unable to locate a company or program that demonstrated scalability at this time. But China's new focus on switchable batteries for electric cars could be a game changer.

I hope that by the time you are reading this, there is much more to report.

Stranded Assets and New Investors for All Fossil Fuels

Nowhere is the complexity of energy more apparent than in the investment arena. Just in the past five years, wind is king, coal is dead. Coal is king, wind is dead. Solar is too expensive; solar is comparable to coal in cost. Natural gas will fix the energy problem cheaply; fracking is the devil incarnate and cannot happen in my backyard. Hydrogen fuel cells, no; electric vehicles, no; biofuels, no; ethanol . . . will fix the transportation problem. The unpredictability, and the cycles of boom and bust, drives investors nuts—not to mention analysts, businesspeople and environmentalists.

Indian industrialist Ratan Tata, chairman of the Tata companies, recently admitted that the energy from his company's new massive coal power plant in India will bring energy to market at roughly the same price as new solar. Tata actually described this plant as a "nonperforming asset" due to the increasing unavailability and high cost of coal.[36] So all of the people, businesses and infrastructure built up to support the coal for this huge power plant are in for a big shock.

In addition to the potential for stranded assets, as in Tata's case, one only has to run some full-cost analysis to see that renewable energy is almost always a cheaper and safer long-term business and government investment option than fossil fuels. This may explain why investment in renewables surpassed fossil fuels in 2011 globally, according to Bloomberg New Energy Finance, reaching a total of $257 billion.[37] At the time, Bloomberg said it also anticipates continued boom growth in the renewable sector over the next twenty years, coming to about $7 trillion. Remember when I said things were changing rapidly? Well, just yesterday in November 2012, Bloomberg New Energy Finance announced that, for the first time in a decade, investments in renewables in 2012 will decrease—by 20 percent. The energy market is subject to a huge variety of factors and policies. Stay tuned.

The real trouble is in the unlikeliest of places: the finances of big oil companies. Current scientific consensus is that any global temperature rise above 2 degrees Celsius will cause climate chaos. But even if only 75 percent of the oil already counted as assets (about $22 trillion) on the books of big oil companies actually were combusted, we would reach a 5-degree Celsius global temperature increase. That will alter all planetary systems and eliminate any safe environment for current models of civilization. Some financial analysts are now calling this a $22 trillion stranded asset problem. It's hard to get one's head around these numbers and these impacts.

John Fullerton, founder and president of the Capital Institute and former managing director at JPMorgan Chase, sums up the next chart very nicely.

[C]ivilization is facing our $20 trillion big choice—our investments or our planet. Recall the direct financial losses of the subprime crisis in the US were a mere $2.7 trillion, and we know what that did. As terrifying as this math is, we must comprehend that the financial ramifications of it, my $20 trillion "big

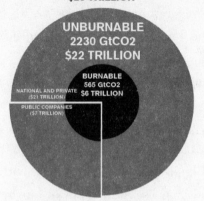

$22 Trillion Carbon Bubble.
Courtesy of Brad Johnson

choice," is only a piece of a more general problem, one I'm calling "financial overshoot." Financial overshoot pits our financial resiliency against our ecological resiliency. Like all arms races, there's no winner here, only hard choices with profound consequences.[38]

This is why I began this chapter with the notion that cost per gallon of gas and cost per kWh of electricity are mere red herrings when it comes to energy policy. Perhaps in the Transition Agenda forums, you and your friends and colleagues and children can design statistical analyses that include common sense, bring to light new solutions and generally help sway public opinion and elected officials and businesses to move on these issues with wartime urgency.

Conclusion

Our future *must* be powered by renewable energy. Several nations and many cities and regions are making extraordinary strides while a diverse group of corporations are moving to net zero carbon energy plans. Other corporations and enormous geopolitical forces are doing everything in their power to prop up and perpetuate a fossil fuel pathway than can only lead to global climate chaos.

Without being dramatic, I have tried to lay out the real choices of 2013 and beyond. The sooner we address these problems with full transparency, the sooner we spend our money and time on building renewable energy infrastructure; viable mass transit; lightweight and high-miles-per-gallon cars; and smart industrial, architectural and land use design. All of our buildings would be outfitted with energy and water efficiency systems, and we'd have a renewable energy grid that is even smarter than our amazingly smart phones. And when naysayers argue that we can never supply our energy demands with renewables and efficiency, note that the percentage of energy in the United States from renewables doubled between 2008 and 2012 to nearly 6 percent, not including hydropower, which brings the percentage up to 12 percent.[39] In Germany, 25 percent of power is supplied by renewable energy.[40]

Stay tuned for some breakthrough technologies across the renewable sector in solar and wave power in particular. Putting turbo boosters under this industry is the *only* prudent thing to do and is a fundamentally conservative view of conserving resources.

Your expertise and personal energy are the only antidotes to bad energy policy. The power is in your hands.

6

EXTREME WEATHER AND THE FOOD/WATER/ ENERGY NEXUS

No serious analyst of climate and weather can dispute the rising cost in lives and property from extreme events. Postponing action increases the consequences and delays appropriate adaptation measures.

—Franklin Nutter, President, Reinsurance Association of America

The topic of extreme weather was originally going to be an addendum to this book. And then the 2012 global drought happened. And then the 2012 heat wave happened. And then Hurricane Sandy happened. Weather took center stage in 2012.

Scientists and environmentalists have been reluctant to point to any given storm or weather event and say it was caused by climate change—until Hurricane Sandy decimated half the East Coast on October 29. Then, on November 1, I heard the following exchange between CNN host Piers Morgan and CNN meteorologist Chad Myers.

PIERS MORGAN: Let's bring somebody who is used to taking the blow, CNN meteorologist Chad Myers. Chad, you've been in this game nearly three decades. Is this global warming that we're seeing? From a meteorological point of view, is there any other explanation?

CHAD MYERS: It is the prime suspect. I don't have another one.[1]

I've used many other people's writings, research and graphics to illustrate this subject, and I thank them for their permission and analysis. Extreme weather affects all human and natural systems, and this chapter strives to briefly describe its impact on literally everything. Food, water and energy are all interdependent, and they all require stable weather systems. Recent and frequent disruptions of these basic needs that we once took for granted are sparking a new appreciation for the dangers of climate change.

Much of today's extreme weather is caused by greenhouse gas emissions largely generated over the last seventy-five years. This long-term effect is the reason for the second Nature Means Business tenet: Take the Long View, which asks that going forward, all financial and environmental actions incorporate future impacts into today's numbers.

But it also lays plain the connection between financial and environmental debt, and Hurricane Sandy is a prime example. I grew up in the Rockaway section of Queens, and it was very hard hit by this late October 2012 storm. Rockaway is a ten-mile-long, very narrow barrier peninsula of New York City, bounded by the Atlantic Ocean and Jamaica Bay. I watched the news, as everyone else did, and then went out to help my cousins clear out waterlogged debris from their house. Both the short- and long-term impacts of the storm quickly became clear. With assistance, most residents will recover within a year—one very tough year.

All the residents of Rockaway will need to move for many months because their houses need major renovations. All the schools are closed indefinitely. Salt water flooded every basement (virtually every house has a basement) and also reached a foot or more into the first floor. This means that every house needs new plumbing, new wiring and new furnaces, and the first floors will have to be gutted so that mold doesn't grow in the walls. Every house will be a construction zone, so even if your second floor was untouched, you cannot live there. Many houses caught fire from downed transmission lines; others were slammed by giant waves and collapsed under the force of the sea. Virtually everyone lost a good deal of their belongings. And because three quarters of the residents of the Rockaways did not evacuate, despite a mandatory evacuation order, their cars were also destroyed when salt water flooded the engines.[2] Most will have to buy new cars.

Multiply this impact by hundreds of thousands of people. This scene is the same in many coastal communities along the northeastern seaboard of North America, plus some big damage inland as well. Communities affected range from the very wealthy (the Hamptons and New Jersey's gold coast) to the solidly middle class (Rockaways), to the very poor (the Red Hook housing projects in Brooklyn). The exact costs are not yet clear. But we know that rebuilding will create two simultaneous financial events:

1. A very unwelcome stimulus package—a huge amount of new construction, materials, jobs, car sales, household goods and sales taxes—most of it financed by the federal government (across several agencies) and insurance and reinsurance companies.
2. The long-term devaluation of coastal real estate along the eastern seaboard. If residents cannot sell their houses or apartments or if they are unable to buy flood insurance because it is too expensive or unavailable, or if the homes go down in value by 20 percent (or more), the loss of real estate wealth and security will be huge.

All money is not created equal. Would you rather federal, state and local governments spend our money *preventing* extreme weather events in the future or on *recovery* from extreme weather? This is not a rhetorical question. This is the *real* financial question that has to enter all debates on public budgets.

If I ran the federal government or an insurance or reinsurance company, I would certainly be advocating for a change in rules and premiums on flood insurance. And asking some deeper, more uncomfortable questions to boot: Do we rebuild these areas? At whose cost? Should the federal government demand that home-owners take on more of the risk? Will flood insurance eventually bankrupt us if hundred-year weather events continue to occur every five years?

If I were a decision maker in the federal government or an insurance or reinsurance company, I'd also be asking how we can immediately lower greenhouse gas emissions to turn around extreme weather trends. Reversing these trends will take at least a generation. Extreme weather is here for the foreseeable future no matter what we do. And it will likely get worse.

Nature Means Business

The *Bloomberg Businessweek* cover story from November 1, 2012, "It's Global Warming, Stupid," by Paul M. Barrett, includes a truly concise description of extreme weather.

> Eric Pooley, senior vice president of the Environmental Defense Fund (and former deputy editor of *Bloomberg Businessweek*), offers a baseball analogy: "We can't say that steroids caused any one home run by Barry Bonds, but steroids sure helped him hit more and hit them farther. Now we have weather on steroids."[3]

The year 2012 was a year of astounding weather. The next map shows global weather and climate anomalies for just one month, September 2012 (pre-Hurricane Sandy). The source is a

U.S. federal agency—NOAA, the National Oceanic and Atmospheric Administration.[4]

And a September 2012 *National Geographic* article shows how extreme weather has been on the rise for the past century—in truly frightening ways[5]:

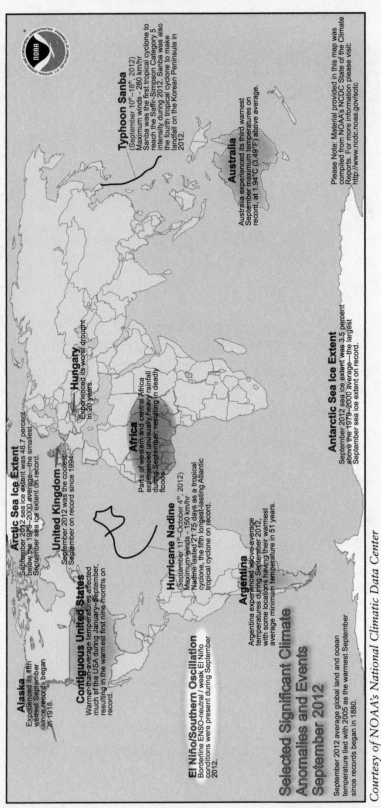

Selected Significant Climate Anomalies and Events September 2012

September 2012 average global land and ocean temperature tied with 2005 as the warmest September since records began in 1880.

Alaska
Experienced its fifth wettest September since records began in 1918.

Contiguous United States
Warmer-than-average temperatures affected much of the USA during January–September, resulting in the warmest first nine months on record.

El Niño/Southern Oscillation
Borderline ENSO-neutral / weak El Niño conditions were present during September 2012.

Argentina
Argentina experienced above-average temperatures during September 2012, with some locations having their warmest average minimum temperature in 51 years.

Hurricane Nadine
(September 11th–October 4th 2012) Maximum winds – 150 km/hr Nadine lasted 21–75 days as a tropical cyclone, the fifth longest-lasting Atlantic tropical cyclone on record.

Arctic Sea Ice Extent
September 2012 sea ice extent was 48.7 percent below the 1979–2000 average—the smallest September sea ice extent on record.

United Kingdom
September 2012 was the coolest September on record since 1994.

Hungary
Experienced its worst drought in 20 years.

Africa
Parts of western and central Africa experienced unusually heavy rainfall during September, resulting in deadly floods.

Typhoon Sanba
(September 10th–18th 2012) Maximum winds – 280 km/hr Sanba was the first tropical cyclone to reach the Saffir-Simpson Category 5 intensity during 2012. Sanba was also the fourth tropical cyclone to make landfall on the Korean Peninsula in 2012.

Australia
Australia experienced its third warmest September maximum temperatures on record, at 1.94°C (3.49°F) above average.

Antarctic Sea Ice Extent
September 2012 sea ice extent was 3.5 percent above the 1979–2000 average—the largest September sea ice extent on record.

Please Note: Material provided in this map was compiled from NOAA's NCDC State of the Climate Reports. For more information please visit: http://www.ncdc.noaa.gov/sotc

Courtesy of NOAA's National Climatic Data Center

WHY SO WILD?

The atmosphere is getting warmer and wetter. Those two trends, which are clear in data averaged globally and annually, are increasing the chances of heat waves, heavy rains, and perhaps other extreme weather.

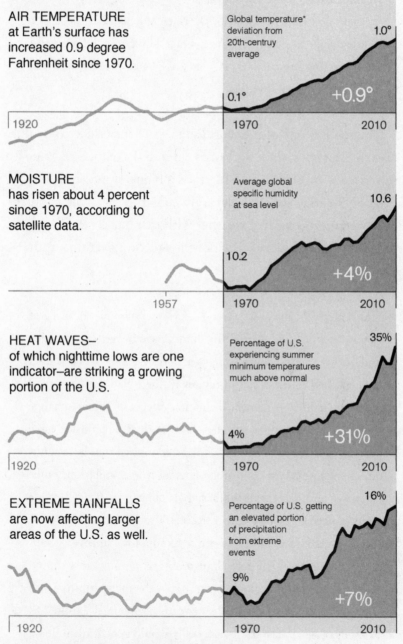

AIR TEMPERATURE at Earth's surface has increased 0.9 degree Fahrenheit since 1970.

Global temperature* deviation from 20th-centruy average

1.0°

0.1°

+0.9°

1920   1970   2010

MOISTURE has risen about 4 percent since 1970, according to satellite data.

Average global specific humidity at sea level

10.6

10.2

+4%

1957   1970   2010

HEAT WAVES– of which nighttime lows are one indicator–are striking a growing portion of the U.S.

Percentage of U.S. experiencing summer minimum temperatures much above normal

35%

4%

+31%

1920   1970   2010

EXTREME RAINFALLS are now affecting larger areas of the U.S. as well.

Percentage of U.S. getting an elevated portion of precipitation from extreme events

16%

9%

+7%

1920   1970   2010

GRAPHS ARE SMOOTHED USING A TEN-YEAR MOVING AVERAGE

*AVERAGE TEMPERATURE OVER LAND AND OCEAN

JOHN TOMANIO, NGM STAFF. ROBERT THOMASON. SOURCES: JEFF MASTERS, WEATHER UNDERGROUND; NATIONAL CLIMATIC DATA CENTER (TEMPERATURE, HEAT WAVES, AND RAINFALL); NOAA (HUMIDITY)

Courtesy of John Tomanio/National Geographic Stock

Rains that are almost biblical, heat waves that don't end, tornadoes that strike in savage swarms—there's been a change in the
weather lately. What's going on?

The atmosphere is getting warmer and wetter. Those two
trends, which are clear in data averaged globally and annually,
are increasing the chances of heat waves, heavy rains, and perhaps other extreme weather.[6]

Munich Re, one of the world's largest reinsurance companies
(Warren Buffett is the company's largest shareholder), issued a
press release in October 2012 titled "North America Most Affected by Weather-Related Natural Catastrophes." The company
directly connects extreme weather with extreme costs. Reinsurers
are the last line of defense before the federal government after a
natural disaster.

The Head of Munich Re's Geo Risks Research unit, Prof. Peter
Höppe, commented: "In all likelihood, we have to regard this
finding as an initial climate-change footprint in our US loss data
from the last four decades. Previously, there had not been such
a strong chain of evidence. If the first effects of climate change
are already perceptible, all alerts and measures against it have
become even more pressing." Höppe continued that even without changing hazard conditions, increases in population, built-
up areas and increasing values, particularly in hazard-prone
regions, need to be on Munich Re's risk radar. All stakeholders
should collaborate and close ranks to support improved adaptation. In addition, climate change mitigation measures should
be supported to limit global warming in the long term to a still
manageable level. "As North America is particularly exposed to
all kinds of weather risks, it especially would benefit from this,"
added Höppe.

Peter Röder, Board member with responsibility for the US market, said: "Climate change-related increases in hazards—unlike increases in exposure—are not automatically reflected in the premiums. In order to realize a sustainable model of insurance, it is crucially important for us as risk managers to learn about this risk of change and find improved solutions for adaptation, but also mitigation. We should prepare for the weather risk changes that lie ahead, and nowhere more so than in North America."[7]

Munich Re calculates the total North American weather disaster losses of 2011 at nearly $150 billion, quadruple the $35 billion of 2001 (though in 2005, Hurricane Katrina spiked to $253 billion). Insured weather losses also quadrupled, from $15 billion in 2001 to $56 billion in 2011, with an interim jump to $116.5 billion for Katrina.[8] The 2012 drought and Hurricane Sandy will most certainly cause the numbers to spike again in 2012.

The next chart shows that, although there is a slight rise in the *number* of weather events over this decade, the real news is the increased *intensity* of the storms. That's what extreme weather means. And extreme weather is both terrifying and bloody expensive.

Connect the dots. The product and profits of Exxon/Mobil and other fossil fuel companies are responsible for a good deal of the costs in the chart above—but those companies did not pay these costs. The rest of us did. Exxon/Mobil made its largest profit ever, $41 billion, in 2011.[9] But its product directly contributed to the cost of extreme weather borne by people, governments and other businesses around the world in the form of pollution, climate change and extreme weather. Only when the price of fossil fuels and other contributors to climate change reflect their true external costs do we stand a chance of moving our economy to safer ground.

Insured losses

In billions of US dollars
2011 values

■ All Events
■ Weather Events

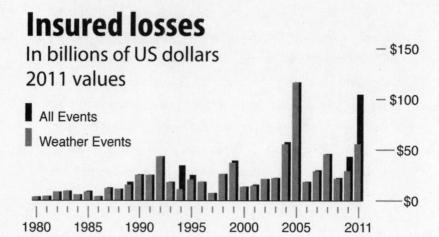

Overall losses

In billions of US dollars
2011 values

■ All Events
■ Weather Events

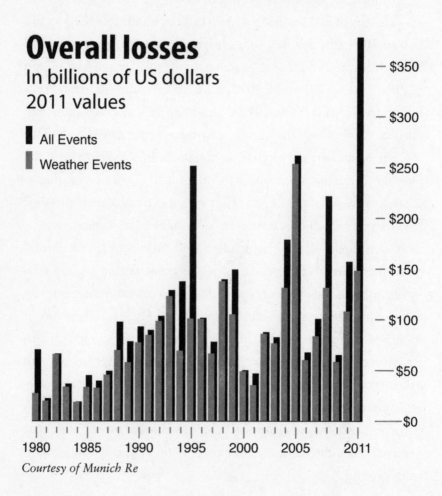

Courtesy of Munich Re

IT WASN'T HIS DRIVING THAT CAUSED THE ALASKAN OIL SPILL. IT WAS YOURS.

It would be easy to blame the Valdez oil spill on one man. Or one company. Or even one industry.

Too easy.

Because the truth is, the spill was caused by a nation drunk on oil. And a government asleep at the wheel.

Did you know that if the government raised efficiency standards for cars just 1 MPG it would save 420,000 barrels of oil a day, or about twice the oil lost in the spill?

And that heat escaping through leaky windows wastes more oil than the Alaskan pipeline supplies in a year?

What it comes down to is this: As long as we are so depen-dent on fossil fuels and so wasteful of the oil we have, more offshore drilling and disastrous oil spills are inevitable.

But together we can curb our dependency on oil.

We can shelve Bush's plan to lease the continental shelf to offshore drillers. We can put pressure on Washington to tighten auto efficiency standards and restore the funding for renewable energy sources Reagan took away.

And we can convince U.S. automakers to stop pushing large cars and muscle cars, and get back to marketing more fuel efficient automobiles.

Support Greenpeace.

Because it's time we put the brakes on our nation's oil dependency.

GREENPEACE

Courtesy of Greenpeace

And we're all in it together. Greenpeace ran a story in its quarterly magazine following the Exxon *Valdez* accident in 1989. (The photo is of the ship's captain, Joseph Hazelwood.) It poignantly notes that we are the users and beneficiaries of Exxon's product. Only when we create incentives for Exxon/Mobil to make its money from products that do not incur environmental debt will it and other fossil fuel companies change their product lines. It's up to us to drive differently, less, and/or different kinds of vehicles as well as commit large public monies to building public transit infrastructure. New car technologies will help, but we cannot wait. This will be a gargantuan effort involving the public, private and individual sectors.

The Food/Water/Energy Nexus

In its Global Trends 2030 December 2012 report, the National Intelligence Council of the U.S. government notes four mega-trends to watch. One is the Food, Water, Energy Nexus. The report notes: "Demand for these resources will grow substantially owing to an increase in the global population. Tackling problems pertaining to one commodity will be linked to supply and demand for the others."[10]

And in a January 2013 *New York Times* article describing the doubling of corn prices in Guatemala over the past three years, Elizabeth Rosenthal describes the problem well: "Recent laws in the United States and Europe that mandate the increasing use of biofuel in cars have had far-flung ripple effects, economists say, as land once devoted to growing food for humans is now sometimes more profitably used for churning out vehicle fuel."[11]

Here's what you need to know about what's in store for these critical and interdependent systems:

- **Extreme weather is the new normal.** And it brings with it huge impacts across the spectrum. It will create incalculable environmental debt.
- **Water scarcity is the new normal.** As glaciers and snow at high altitudes disappear due to warmer weather, less fresh water flows down to watersheds. Water is needed for survival, agriculture and energy.
- **Food price unpredictability is the new normal.** As weather regularly swings outside of its historical pendulum, it's harder and harder to plan for both large and small agriculture. It is also harder for all businesses that use agricultural products to project earnings.
- **Energy price, availability and unpredictability are the new normal.** Energy is needed for water and food production and delivery.

Hence the fragility of the food/water/energy nexus.

The bright side is that positive effects are multiplied in the same way as negatives. For instance, renewable energy's light touch on water supplies adds to its advantages. And you don't have to be a survivalist or locavore to appreciate the convenience and taste of localized food options as well as their sustainability. That is why cities from Seattle to Detroit are looking at ways to increase and incentivize urban agriculture.

The Ripple Effects of Water Scarcity

In the direst cases, a region might have to decide whether to use its water for coal or nuclear energy or food. In fact, India had to make that choice during its summer drought in 2012, and 650 million people endured rolling blackouts when the government chose to use water for food rather than energy. This impossible choice should no longer seem out of the question to Americans, who suffered their own drought at the same time.

And as a recent report on the connection between water and energy from HSBC, the world's third largest bank with total assets of $2.6 trillion, notes, "Cities like Beijing and farming heartlands are at risk of water shortages from China's surging demand for power." The report is titled "No Water, No Power: Is there enough water to fuel China's power expansion?"[12] HSBC and other major financial institutions are watching and worrying as shortages loom.

A Greenpeace Africa report sums up the water/energy conflict succinctly: "Coal can be replaced, water can't."[13]

Political security is threatened when water disappears. Fifty nations attended a United Nations event in 2012 called "Water, Peace and Security," where the U.S. State Department issued a public briefing, "Global Water Security, US Intelligence Community Assessment" and the InterAction Council, led by thirty former heads of state, released "The Global Water Crisis: Addressing an Urgent Security Issue." In the document, Secretary of State

Hillary Clinton warned that water could become a source of tension between countries causing "state failure" as the level of water tension rises.[14]

I was recently in a meeting with oil company executives where several broached the idea that the impact of fuels should be measured based on carbon and national security separately. We were discussing new fuel sources, and the oil company executives advocated for expanded drilling in the Arctic and importing of Canadian tar sands through a cross-continental U.S. pipeline. They based their advocacy on national security versus curtailing carbon as the primary benchmark. As I pointed out at that meeting, reducing carbon emissions *is* national security. Executives from several iconic multinational companies echoed my opinion. The divergence of interests again represents the fissure in the business world.

> The foot bone connected to the ankle bone,
>
> The ankle bone connected to the shin bone,
>
> The shin bone connected to the knee bone,
>
> The knee bone connected to the thigh bone,
>
> The thigh bone connected to the hip bone,
>
> The hip bone connected to the back bone,
>
> The back bone connected to the shoulder bone,
>
> The shoulder bone connected to the neck bone,
>
> The neck bone connected to the head bone,
>
> Them bones got up and walked around
>
> —James Weldon Johnson, based on Ezekiel 37:1

Extreme weather makes all of our systems dysfunctional. Droughts, floods and heat waves destroy crops, energy and water sources. Intense storms destroy whole regions and infrastructure. All of it costs untold amounts of money, and our only option is to radically decrease greenhouse gas emissions.

We know from history that the public, private and individual sectors can all achieve the unimaginable. Climate change is the defining issue of the twenty-first century. If our weather system does not support our economic system, nothing works. That's why we need innovations like those outlined in chapter 7. If ever there was another time to shoot for the moon, this is it.

7

THE CUTTING EDGE
OF INNOVATION

IN THE LAB,
THE EXECUTIVE SUITE,
THE HALLS OF CONGRESS
AND THE PATENT OFFICE

nnovation is one of those words that gets bandied about so much that its meaning gets awfully diluted. But when you catch the real thing, it's absolutely thrilling. Just as the accountants of chapter 3 are revolutionaries in suits, there are scientists, engineers, entrepreneurs, investors and blue-collar workers lighting up the world—literally. Occasionally even government officials enact policies that encourage progress as well as profit.

This chapter highlights a handful of innovations that could unleash a huge amount of renewable energy, spark the twenty-first century's industrial development and help build a foundation for global security. They range from biomimicry, one of the coolest areas in scientific research, with countless industrial applications; to new intellectual property rules that allow collaboration to coexist with competition; a public/private initiative that marries solar power, electric vehicles and public infrastructure spending. We'll also look at some surprising new profit centers, where one person's garbage (or excretions) is another person's gold. And we'll see how tax incentives for green technology could double as both financial lubricants and foreign policy carrots to make global environmental treaties more palatable across the board. Some of these innovations are already under way, others are still pipe dreams.

In the Laboratory: Biomimicry

The best ideas are those that seem obvious *after* someone thinks of them. Of course. Why didn't I think of that? It was staring us in the face. Biomimicry is one of those ideas. Rather than try to summarize the concept myself, I'll defer to its founding leader, Janine Benyus, in her phenomenal 1997 book *Biomimicry: Innovation Inspired by Nature.*

> Luckily for us, our planet-mates—the fantastic meshwork of plants, animals, and microbes—have been patiently perfecting their wares since an incredible 3.8 billion years since the first bacteria. In that time, life has learned to fly, circumnavigate the globe, live in the depths of the ocean and atop the highest peaks, craft miracle materials, light up the night, lasso the sun's energy, and build a self-reflective brain. Collectively, organisms have managed to turn rock and sea into a life-friendly home, with steady temperatures and smoothly percolating cycles. In short, living things have done everything we want to do, without guzzling fossil fuel, polluting the planet, or mortgaging their future. What better models could there be?
>
> . . . I call their quest biomimicry—the conscious emulation of life's genius. Innovation inspired by nature.
>
> In a society accustomed to dominating or "improving" nature, this respectful imitation is a radically new approach, a revolution really. Unlike the Industrial Revolution, the Biomimicry

Revolution introduces an era based not on what we can extract from nature, but on what we can learn from her.

As you will see, "doing it nature's way" has the potential to change the way we grow food, make materials, harness energy, heal ourselves, store information, and conduct business.

In a biomimetic world, we would manufacture the way animals and plants do, using sun and simple compounds to produce totally biodegradable fibers, ceramics, plastics, and chemicals. Our farms, modeled on prairies, would be self-fertilizing and pest-resistant. To find new drugs or crops, we would consult animals and insects that have used plants for millions of years to keep themselves healthy and nourished. Even computing would take its cue from nature, with software that "evolves" solutions, and hardware that uses the lock-and-key paradigm to compute by touch."[1]

Wow. Since Janine wrote this treatise, biomimicry has become a major force at the nexus of science and business. Regional groups dedicated to the concept have recently sprung up all over the world, including Mexico, South Africa, Europe and Asia, and there are eight in the United States alone. (Full disclosure: I am the chair of the Biomimicry NYC Advisory Board.) These new groups will help educate businesses, scientists and local governments about this promising new approach. After his first biomimicry workshop, the lead engineer of a consumer goods giant noted that even though he'd been developing products for thirty-five years, he'd never taken a toxicology course. He then enrolled his entire research and development division in a three-day biomimicry workshop. Many other multinationals are pursuing the same kind of internal reeducation.

A handful of pioneers have been working in green chemistry for decades, such as InterfaceFLOR, the world's largest carpet and tile company. The late Ray Anderson, Interface's founder, described the company's mission beautifully: "By definition, we are the world's largest designer and maker of carpet tile. By reputation, we are a company of ideas and courage. We stand for sustainability. In 1994 we began to change the way we do business, and the result has been transformational. For us, for the industry. We believe that some companies feel a sense of responsibility larger than the products they sell. That for some companies, design has become a calling so central to their mission it is now second nature. On both fronts, Interface is that company."[2]

Using biomimicry, the company developed more and more sophisticated products. It studied the nonuniform pattern of the forest floor to develop Entropy®, a carpet tile that allows for variations in color quality and texture so that off-spec batches still can be used. As a result, manufacturing waste declined from 4 percent to 1.5 percent, and customers experienced 70 percent less installation waste; plus, Interface no longer needed to back-stock identical replacement tiles. Entropy quickly became the company's most popular product. By 2009, fifteen years after Entropy was introduced, Interface had eliminated 200 million pounds of waste and $433 million in handling costs. Every year, Americans alone throw away about 2 billion pounds of carpet waste, almost none of it biodegradable. So this was a huge accomplishment.

Next, Interface engineers studied how geckos hang from the ceiling, seemingly untouched by gravity. From these observations they developed TacTile® technology, which holds tiles to each other rather than having to glue the tiles directly to the floor. Again, sounds simple—the larger the mass, the greater gravity's effect. With many tiles joined together, the carpet itself creates most of the adhesiveness. This eliminates damage to flooring when the carpet is removed and also eliminates off-gassing of toxic glue chemicals.

Anderson's approach to business has yielded huge benefits for Interface. His successor, chief executive Daniel Hendrix, recently told Tom Randall of Bloomberg, "Our financials would be not nearly as good as they are today if we had not gone down this road. Our products would be more expensive, our talent base would be less, and engagement would be not as good. We would not have as many sales, first of all. One of our biggest customer bases is the architectural design community, and we've gotten a lot of goodwill around sustainability. Also, any time Interface posts a job, people will take a lesser compensation to come work for Interface, just because of the sustainability and higher purpose."[3]

Indeed, biomimicry is a potential game-changer. Perhaps most exciting is the biomimetic approach to solar energy. Scientists and engineers are developing a new energy technology using the lessons of photosynthesis of plants—converting solar energy to chemical energy by splitting water molecules to release hydrogen. These new solar cells might reach the market in 2013. The Bio-mimicry Guild's Ask Nature website describes the process in this way: "Plant-inspired solar cells mimic photosynthetic dyes and processes to generate solar energy many times more cheaply than silicon-based photovoltaics, while having the flexibility to be integrated with a building skin. Conventional silicon-based solar panels capture, separate, and transport light energy in one highly-purified material whose manufacture requires large amounts of energy, toxic solvents, and bulky infrastructure to support rigid panels."[4]

In Japan, the chief engineer of the West Japan Railway Company used his passion for bird watching to help redesign a very high-profile product. The company's bullet train was fabulously fast, but it was so loud that every time the train emerged from a tunnel, residents as far as a half mile away complained of thunder claps. The chief engineer remembered that the kingfisher dives very quickly and makes barely any noise. Inspired by the shape and movement of the kingfisher's beak, engineers created a new train that was not only quieter but also went 10 percent faster *and* used 15 percent less energy. Equally important for the railway company, it solved a public relations nightmare. The chief engineer's avid bird watching paid off.

Perhaps the best-known example of a biomimicry-inspired product is Velcro, developed in 1941. The inventor, George de Mestral, removed burrs from his dog and decided to figure out how they worked. Why were they so hard to remove? He found tiny hooks on the end of the burrs' spines that caught anything in their clutches. The two-part Velcro system we all know re-creates this natural reversible stickiness and is now used in countless applications.

Another biomimicry-inspired innovation being deployed more and more is passive air conditioning. Biologists and engineers have studied termite mounds, which can keep a certain temperature no matter what is going on outside, and architects are designing buildings inspired by these structures (minus the termites, obviously). In many of these new buildings, air conditioning is not needed even in very hot climates. From the Biomimicry website: "The termites achieve this remarkable feat by constantly opening and closing a series of heating and cooling vents throughout the mound over the course of the day. With a system of carefully adjusted convection currents, air is sucked in at the lower part of the mound, down into enclosures with muddy walls, and up through a channel to the peak of the termite mound."[5]

Yes, this is the future. Today there are hundreds of examples of biomimicry at work . . . and likely there are architects, designers, schools, industrial companies and governments near you embracing the approach.

Infrastructure and Policy That Solve
Several Problems at Once

Shai Agassi, a successful Silicon Valley entrepreneur, was asked the right questions at the right time by the right people. In 2005, he attended Young Global Leaders, an invitation-only group for politicians and businesspeople under the age of forty. At the meeting, World Economic Forum head Klaus Schwab asked the group to think about how to "make the world a better place" by 2020. Shai's assignment was the environment, and he focused on climate change. The more he learned, the more obsessed he became. He zeroed in on the automobile and read everything he could get his hands on. Then in 2006, Shimon Peres of Israel (former prime minister and then a minister for business development) asked Shai, "How could you run a country without oil?" You don't have to be as smart as Shai to understand that this was not an idle question. Shai's answer was breathtaking in both its simplicity and foresight. He separated the battery from the electric car, now called the switchable battery.

And six years later, in 2012, his start-up, Better Place, sold its first cars in Israel and Denmark.[6] The cars, standard midsize sedans, are manufactured by Nissan-Renault. There's only one model now (pick your color), but that will change in 2013.[7]

Better Place executes its technological and infrastructure innovations with the goal of transforming private automobile transportation. Why try for small changes when we need big ones? Shai's original white paper outlining his vision conceived it as a government infrastructure project. After some back-and-forth, Peres convinced Shai to leave German multinational technology company SAP (which had bought his software company for $400 million a few years earlier and where he was being groomed for the top job) and become an entrepreneur again. Better Place became a for-profit corporation in 2007, and within two months, it raised $200 million from a broad group of investors. It was a record first investment round for a clean-tech start-up.

Better Place has four significant innovations: cars with removable/switchable battery cassettes; the smart batteries themselves; gas station infrastructure equipped with charging and replacement capacity for the battery cassettes; and sophisticated consumer-facing and back-end software.

Basically, instead of refilling with gasoline, a driver exchanges a depleted or low-on-energy cassette with a fully charged one in the same time it would take to refuel. The battery-charging stations are powered by renewable energy (solar and wind).

Better Place cars are actually cheaper than comparable gas-burning cars. In fact, the company is as much an energy company as it is a car company. Its business model contributes to the supply of and demand for renewable energy, encouraging the further development of that sector. It also offers the sensible, integrated view of transportation and its side effects (good and bad) that must inform twenty-first-century business and investment. Its ambitions are astonishing.

As the global gas price chart in chapter 5 showed, the price of gas is higher pretty much everywhere in the world than it is the United States. This is a huge roadblock for Better Place when it comes to the U.S. market. The high price of gas is part of the Better Place business model and is what makes the vehicles cheap for global consumers. But they would still be more expensive than their competition in the United States if gas prices remain as they are.

Better Place opened a showroom in Tel Aviv in February 2010 and one in Copenhagen in March 2011. Within a year, about 110,000 people had visited to see the new cars. That's a lotta people coming to see a midsize sedan. Most significantly, Better Place signed its first contract in 2012 with the second largest utility in China to bring switchable battery electric cars to the world's largest auto market.[8] Electric vehicles are one of the seven pillars of China's new Five Year Plan, and the country intends to create the international standard for switchable batteries. Better Place is the company developing both the experience and the frontier technology.

Better Place's technology is a triumph, at once very sophisticated and very user friendly. The Global Positioning System (GPS) on Better Place cars tells you your route, where you can switch your battery *and* how much battery power is left in the car for how many miles according to your destination. Each driver has a personal code that he or she enters before starting the car, so if a husband drives like he cannot afford to ever get another speeding ticket—at a steady 55 miles per hour—and his wife drives at 75 miles per hour, the GPS will adjust its info on how far the car can go based on driving patterns, including current traffic conditions.

Better Place's goal is to fulfill Shimon Peres's vision: to enable Israel and the rest of the world to live without oil by 2020. Israel has a few distinguishing characteristics that make this target more achievable than it would be elsewhere. First, it's a small country where very few people drive long distances on a regular basis. This means less pressure on Better Place to build out infrastructure than it would face in, say, Arizona. Second, Israel enjoys three hundred days of sunshine a year and already has a concentration of renewable energy technology companies. This allows for a strong solar industry and other technological innovators with which Better Place can work to develop the infrastructure. And most important, Israel's government understands viscerally the need to eliminate a dependence on oil for reasons that have nothing to do with the environment.

The jury is still out on whether Better Place's business is going to be scalable and profitable. And in October 2012, Shai was removed as chief executive by the board for the public reason that he is a start-up entrepreneur and the company now needed a corporate veteran. Whoever is at the helm, one can only hope that the company achieves its revolutionary goals.

All governments should be asking themselves the same question: How can we live without oil?

Garbage to Gold: The Next Wave of Recycling

> Too much garbage in your face? There's plenty of space out in space!
>
> —From the movie *WALL-E*

There's another trend going on. As landfill and transport prices go up and places to dump garbage become scarce and farther afield, a new view of recycling has emerged. Paper, plastic and cans are one thing—but suddenly yard waste, food, compostable matter, used frying oil and in some places even urine and feces (both animal and human) are becoming valuable commodities in new cycles of usage. This trend is environmentally sound and also financially necessary for the long haul.

Here are some statistics to contemplate on the composition of our garbage from the Clean Air Council.[9]

Every year, Americans use the equivalent of 300 million 100-foot-tall Douglas fir trees in paper and wood products (that's one tree for each of us). We throw away enough paper and plastic cups, forks and spoons to circle the equator three hundred times. Every year, Americans use approximately 1 billion nonbiodegradable plastic shopping bags, creating 300,000 tons of landfill waste.

Less than 1 percent of these bags are recycled each year.

And unfortunately, the pricing incentives for recycling are all screwed up. Recycling 1 ton of plastic bags costs $4,000, but the recycled product can be sold for only $32. Glass, metal and plastic recycling costs New York City $240 per ton, almost twice what it costs to just throw it away. These bad pricing signals epitomize short-term thinking. After all, recycling is an attempt to avert two long-term problems: Where to put all of our garbage? And what will it do to the land, air and water around it? Landfill costs are dangerously underpriced today; as a result, one day soon, they will either have to close or double or triple in price overnight.

But what happens when you make people pay for the costs of trash disposal is striking. Where landfill costs *have* risen, recycling and composting rates have gone through the roof.

For example, after Ireland created a 15-cent charge per plastic bag in 2002, bag consumption dropped by 90 percent. In 2008, the average person in Ireland used 27 plastic bags, while the average person in Britain used 220. And as a bonus, the Irish program has raised millions of euros in revenue.

Recycling 1 ton of mixed paper saves the energy equivalent of 185 gallons of gasoline.

Recycling 1 ton of aluminum cans conserves more than 207 million British thermal units (Btus), which is equal to 36 barrels of oil or 1,665 gallons of gasoline.

The recycling rate of 32.5 percent in the United States in 2006 saved the carbon emission equivalent of taking 39.4 million cars off the road. Individual commitment paired with good policy *can* actually yield valuable progress.[10]

Let's look at a community-specific example. The Nova Scotia Provincial Government chose to enact a serious waste reduction program starting in 1995 to address concerns over water and air pollution from landfills and waste incinerators.[11] I vacation every summer in a Nova Scotia cottage, and the first year I went, 1999, there was barely recycling of any kind. By 2002, there was recycling of cans, glass, plastic and paper alongside normal garbage pickup.[12] Today 99 percent of Nova Scotians have curbside recycling. As of 2012, each house is only allowed one bag of normal garbage per family every two weeks but unlimited amounts of compost and recycling.

This organic compost output has increased 35-fold in the past fifteen years. And the Nova Scotia Government then sells the compost for $34.50 a ton, primarily to residential and horticultural markets, with residents entitled to 220 pounds of compost for free each year.[13] The compost market, its collection and the resulting products are becoming more sophisticated as the need for modern waste disposal becomes clearer and clearer. Compost is used for fertilizer and soil conditioner and as a natural pesticide. The province's program is recognized as a leader in this field, and the local government believes it can eliminate another quarter of its nonrecyclable and noncompostable waste by 2015. In a world with Nature Means Business rules, this kind of policy would always save money as well as the environment.

In Seattle, there are similarly strict restrictions on garbage. A household has to pay for anything over a small garbage bag per week. No municipality can really afford big landfill costs, and the more aggressive the restrictions, the more effective they are as cost controls. Not only is this just good policy, but it engages citizens in keeping their communities more financially and environmentally secure. It is the individual sector at work again. And the zoos also. Seattle's Woodland Park Zoo sells ZooDoo Compost.[14] The most "poopular" compost in the Pacific Northwest, the zoo's nearly 1 million pounds of compost each year saves $60,000 in annual disposal costs plus brings in sizable revenues. New Zealand's Zoo calls its compost program "the number one for number two."[15]

The relationship between urine and feces and human health is pretty clear. What goes in must be clean and what goes out must be safely disposed of, while protecting nearby water and land. The Gates Foundation, as part of its Global Health Initiative, is calling for a "toilet revolution." It has given $400,000 to eight universities to come up with a better bowl.[16] The toilets must be hygienic and sustainable, discharge no pollutants, generate energy, recover nutrients, use only a tiny amount of water and cost only a nickel per person per day. Stay tuned for the results.

A Urinetown scenario is not crazy to imagine, given the droughts afflicting large parts of the world. In fact, urine and feces

Sticking with bodily functions, in 2001, there was a Broadway musical called *Urinetown,* perhaps the first environment-themed Broadway musical. (There have been many such plays but no musicals.) The show takes place after a twenty-year drought, and the lyrics to the song "It's a Privilege to Pee" tell the story.

It's a privilege to pee
Water's worth its weight
In gold these days

No more bathrooms
Like in olden days
You come here and pay a fee
For the privilege to pee

Twenty years we've had the drought
And our reservoirs have all dried up
I take my baths now in a coffee cup
I boil what's left of it for tea
And it's a privilege to pee

contain nutrients that can be used in different ways. The big trick is to separate them from each other; don't be surprised if you hear about urine diversion toilets in the next few years. Urine, because it is sterile and low in pathogens, speeds up the breakdown of compost for fertilizer. Feces is currently being developed as a biofuel in the laboratory. Better to ride on your own horsepower than have to send it to expensive sewage treatment.

Back on the eating end of the cycle, used frying oil from restaurants and leftover fat from animal rendering plants both now comprise a growing business—there have even been reports of theft and bribery. Biodiesel is a good alternative to normal diesel fuel or heating oil. In fact, Rudolf Diesel's first model engine, built in 1893, ran on nothing but peanut oil.

Currently, biodiesel is made from a variety of sources, including virgin oils (usually soybean by-products), used cooking grease, leftover fats from animal rendering plants and algae. By the time you read this, there will likely be new source materials on the market.

Biodiesel from waste material reduces greenhouse gas emissions from combustion engines by 60 to 80 percent, making it very hard to beat as a new source of fuel. But as explained in chapter 6, there is a real competition between diverting agriculture for food to agriculture for fuel. This issue will remain contentious for the coming decade.

Restaurants and animal rendering plants used to have to pay to dispose of their used grease and leftover lard.[17] Now there is a booming market for these fats, which command about 40 cents per pound, and even a corresponding black market. Theft of these fats is becoming so widespread that several U.S. states have enacted new statutes to regulate grease collection—an industry Tony Soprano would love. One California company, Sacramento Rendering, reported 50,000 pounds of raw grease stolen per week—worth a tidy $750,000 a year.

Government has the opportunity to create incentives and costs at every step of the value chain, so that someday all garbage might be viewed as gold. Doing this would spur new business development and greatly reduce the environmental debt incurred by elimination of all kinds.

Patent Pooling: Innovation at the Negotiating Table

In 2011, President Obama committed an unprecedented and controversial $15 billion of government money for R&D in renewable energies. (This number is likely much higher if you count defense spending, but that budget is more difficult to assess.) That's a start. However, the prospect of climate change deserves a response commensurate with its consequences—that is, a wartime response. When President Franklin Roosevelt took America into World War II, he set tremendously audacious goals for industry and also called for national sacrifice to support the military effort. Although many Americans bristled at this, in hindsight, it is clear that this wartime effort not only enabled the Allied defeat of fascism but also created America's postwar technological and industrial dominance. If current government policy (all governments, not just American) prioritized renewable energy as the U.S. government prioritized military manufacturing in 1941, the world would quickly see a revolution in renewable energy technologies. And that's exactly the type of revolution needed to quickly transition out of fossil fuel dependence.

Here's the premise: Those investing in innovation should get a proper share of the spoils. Energy companies must either innovate to dramatically lower fossil fuel dependence or be replaced by companies that do. If you count the increased costs of extreme weather due to climate change, the costs of these intense efforts would not seem extraordinary. Rather, they are appropriate to the problem.

Times of crisis often call for a change in format, to spur inspiration and innovation. Patent pooling, an agreement between two or more companies to cross-license patents, has been around since the nineteenth century. Since then it has spawned numerous technological breakthroughs. For simplicity's sake, I've named this new iteration of the concept PROTECT (*p*atent-pooling *r*einforcement for *t*ransformative *e*nvironmental and *c*lean *t*echnologies).

The purpose of PROTECT is to get the best scientists working together on renewable energy breakthroughs as well as to protect the interests of corporations that invest in this crucial R&D. I designed this concept originally in frustration as I learned about the brilliant work being done in laboratories of both General Electric and IBM. I wanted to scream, "This is an emergency, please work together." So I got to thinking. I designed PROTECT from the U.S. perspective as a case study, but of course international participation would be ideal. It's a pillar of a Transition Agenda outlined in chapter 8. Your advocacy and intelligence are the keys to urging companies and governments to cooperate in new ways to fast-track new technologies to market. Twenty percent of a huge breakthrough can be as lucrative or better than 100 percent of a piece of a partial one.

The challenges to energy independence are twofold: storage (for when the sun doesn't shine and the wind doesn't blow) and dissemination. Wind and solar power are out there for the taking, but the technology to harness this limitless power can't yet satisfy demand, even after recent dramatic improvements in efficiency. How to translate the offshore winds of Massachusetts into a reliable power source for Boston? Where to store the heat from the California sun so that Los Angeles can light up on solar power? Better storage and dissemination will pave the path to energy independence—an urgent need for every modern economy.

Greater storage capacity is the biggest challenge, and a unified "smart grid" to plug in and connect decentralized power production from renewable energy sources could be initiated today. Scientists in large corporations, tiny start-ups, universities and government labs are tackling these problems. Whoever gets there first stands to profit immensely. That's capitalism at work. But this current model is too slow because climate chaos is literally knocking at the door—we see it in every day's global weather reports and agricultural news.

The uptake of renewable energy must imitate the speed of the computer and Internet revolution. Cisco didn't exist until 1984; Amazon, 1995; Google, 1998; Facebook, 2004; and Twitter,

2006.[18] Apple and Microsoft both started in 1976. We need a similar turnaround time for the energy revolution. The same is true for transportation. The combustion engine fueled by petroleum must be replaced. These challenges are extraordinary, but considering the (very partial) list of companies that didn't even exist a generation ago, we must remember how fast business can transform the world—especially when it has smart government policy to back it up.

It's not enough to hand out grants and R&D money to corporations and universities. *All* government grants and subsidies are subject to political pressure, and in the name of long-term self-interest and lowering our environmental debt, we must demand a different format. Patent pooling offers a framework for competing companies and academic institutions to collaborate without risking loss.

A 2000 publication from the U.S. Patent and Trademark Office describes several historical efforts at patent pooling.[19] Over the last 150 years, patent pools have played an important role in shaping both the industry and the law in the United States. In 1856, for example, the Sewing Machine Combination formed one of the first patent pools consisting of sewing machine patents. In 1917, as a result of a recommendation of a committee formed by the assistant secretary of the navy (the Honorable Franklin D. Roosevelt), an aircraft patent pool was privately formed encompassing almost all aircraft manufacturers in the United States. The creation of the Manufacturer's Aircraft Association was crucial to the U.S. government because the two major patent holders, the Wright Company and the Curtiss Company, had effectively blocked the building of any new airplanes, which were desperately needed as the United States was entering World War I. In 1924, an organization first named the Associated Radio Manufacturers and later the Radio Corporation of America (RCA) merged the radio interests of American Marconi, General Electric, American

Telephone and Telegraph (AT&T) and Westinghouse, leading to the establishment of standardization of radio parts, airway frequency locations and television transmission standards. A more recent patent pool was formed in 1997 by the Trustees of Columbia University, Fujitsu Limited, General Instrument Corp., Lucent Technologies Inc., Matsushita Electric Industrial Co., Ltd., Mitsubishi Electric Corp., Philips Electronics N.V. (Philips), Scientific Atlanta, Inc. and Sony Corp. (Sony) to jointly share royalties from patents that are essential to compliance with the MPEG2 compression technology standard. In 1999, nine companies joined together to acquire a patent joint license for digital video disks.

For the future of the economy as well as the planet, we need a fresh program to shake up energy research. Currently, constraints exist on all private and public budgets, largely due to lingering debt, a shaky global economy and a public aversion to paying taxes for government services. As environmental debt becomes more understood as a multiplier of this financial debt, we have a chance to address both issues at once. Here is some background and a first template for PROTECT.

Government Funding, Private Scientists

There are precedents where government has instigated, funded and catalyzed new technologies.

When the United States decided it needed the ultimate weapon against Hitler, it brought together the world's top scientists and funded their technological breakthroughs via the Manhattan Project. It spared no money and it spared no scientists. And whatever you think of the creation and deployment of the atom bomb, the weapon changed the course of history.

During the cold war, when the U.S. government decided to reach for the moon in a decade, it spent $20 billion in ten years (approximately $150 billion in 2012 dollars).[20] The world's best scientists were brought to the task, and Apollo touched down six months early. Today's ambitions must be of comparable sizes, as the task is arguably even more important to national security.

The main difference between past efforts and today's is that many companies, universities and investors have already begun seeking the big breakthrough for storage capacity—perhaps in a new iteration of the battery. The U.S. government, through the Department of Defense (the Defense Advanced Research Projects Agency), the Department of Energy (National Renewable Energy Labs) and other agencies, provides a variety of funding grants and initiatives. But until now, the majority of the funding has come from private individuals or corporations.

Many corporations invest and work on energy technologies with a sense of urgency, for obvious reasons. However, patent rules require the best scientists from IBM and the best scientists from GE to keep their ideas from each other until they're patented. And why shouldn't they? These parent companies are financing the basic R&D and expect to be rewarded accordingly. They should be. But in the truly long view, companies would be better positioned if they solved basic technological issues together and shared proportionate to each company's investment in the (presumably greater) spoils. After all, within a decade, whoever is leading this innovation will be such a powerful force that a little shared credit couldn't hurt them.

PROTECT would merge these interests and convene a broad array of scientists, engineers and inventors, with the parties sharing the royalties on a pro rata basis. Government could be a co-investor, but its most important function would be to create and uphold a framework for protecting each party's interests while also advancing the crucial mission.

Several other versions of this kind of collaboration are already under way. For example, IBM is partnering on R&D for energy sustainability with EDF, the largest electricity producer in Europe. Goldman Sachs created a fund for a "research pool" to help pharmaceutical companies with their individual R&D costs as they develop new drugs. Across industries, there are research collaborations. I am an advisor to the "Sustainability in a Generation" initiative housed at the University of California at Davis's Agricultural Sustainability Institute. The purpose is to design, decipher and disseminate the most promising technologies and practices for agricultural commodity sourcing. The initiative is funded by Mars and a few others, but about a dozen corporations and a dozen NGOs are participating. And the findings will be publicly available.

The Semiconductor Industry: A Precedent to Emulate

The popular view of the technology revolution in Silicon Valley supposes an organic outgrowth of garage inventors, Stanford University, Department of Defense contracts and a few private funders and start-up corporations. Scientists played music together at the local bar and moved from company to company pollinating their ideas and knowledge.

The truth is, in the early days, the revolution needed some help. In the early 1980s, the U.S. semiconductor industry was being clobbered by its Japanese competitors. In response, in 1987, business leaders and the U.S. government created Sematech (Semiconductor Manufacturing Technology), a research consortium of fourteen companies whose mission statement is "to provide the U.S. semiconductor industry the capability for world leadership in manufacturing."[21] Sematech's original fourteen members included many of the nation's leading industrial firms. Several had begun collaborating earlier to combat their loss of market share. This marriage of government and private funding helped lay the groundwork for the wave of innovation that is now synonymous with Silicon Valley.

This model continues in this industry—in Japan. In December 2011, six Japanese companies created a joint venture to develop new semiconductor technology.[22] Mobile operator NTT Docomo recruited five partners—Samsung, Panasonic, Fujitsu Limited, Fujitsu Semiconductor and NEC—to develop and sell chips for mobile devices. Currently the U.S. corporation Qualcomm makes the majority of chips found in smart phones, so this is a sensible response to market pressures.

Expanding this R&D cooperation to include foreign companies and governments would be even more productive. The negotiations would be tough at this moment of international financial insecurity and growing trade protectionism. But it's exactly what a wartime response would look like. And all of these precedents demonstrate that cooperation could fast-track the research for the storage and dissemination of renewable energy. What are we waiting for?!

Green Tax Incentives Can Double as Foreign Policy Tools

In United Nations global climate negotiations, one of the biggest obstacles to a deal is called technology transfer. You might have heard, for instance, that at the 2009 UN Copenhagen Climate talks, the BASIC (Brazil, South Africa, India, China) countries proposed $100 billion for "tech transfer" as part of a potential global deal.[23]

Tech transfer is the money that industrialized economies promise to pay to developing economies to cover the price differential of goods and services if carbon is expensed into manufacturing and transport. When a price for carbon is included, goods become more expensive. This is a crucial consideration for those next billion people in the developing world on the verge of becoming middle class and looking to purchase their first manufactured products. Their governments don't want to sign *anything* that will limit or diminish the ability of their people to enter the next economic tier. Tech transfer subsidies would allow emerging economies to buy and deploy state-of-the-art low-carbon technologies instead of older, cheaper, dirtier ones. Of course the developed world resents having to pay for this tech transfer, especially in an era when wealthier industrialized countries are feeling financially threatened while China, India and Brazil are booming.

Even though China is now the largest contributor to global warming per annum, the United States, Australia, Germany and other Western economies far outpace China on a per-capita basis. So, when we ask those who are just now getting all the stuff we already have to limit their consumption or to pay the full and fair cost of goods, they get really angry. To accurately picture how fast the carbon load in the atmosphere is increasing, consider this: China now emits more greenhouse gas than the United States and Canada *combined*. Fifteen years ago, China was barely on the greenhouse gas map. Most of these new emissions come from the manufacturing of the cheap goods that China then exports to us. It's all one big, interconnected circle of environmental, social and financial considerations.

Developing countries pose a very simple question to the industrialized economies: "You caused these grave environmental problems, and you are already saturated with refrigerators, computers, telephones, houses, cars and air conditioners, all of which you bought with no thought to a price for carbon. Why should we have to pay the full costs of this stuff when you didn't?" (See chapter 3 and externalities.)

One option is for industrialized countries to use green tax incentives for a dual purpose: to spur investment in green technology and to help ameliorate the tech transfer dilemma. Here's one possible solution.

While I was working for Greenpeace as solutions director, I thought there could be common ground between global negotiations on climate change and the large green R&D and infrastructure investments that multinational corporations were making in developing countries. And I was always looking for ways to speed up and incentivize these investments.

What if American corporations received special tax incentives for the extra money they spent on deploying clean technology in the developing world and then put those corporate tax savings into the U.S. tech transfer pot? Everybody would win. The same could work for German, Canadian or Japanese corporations. The goal would be to advance clean technology cheaply and efficiently while creating tax incentives that spur environmental progress. Additionally, because the Securities and Exchange Commission now demands that corporations account for their climate change risk, these investments in the developing world would contribute to the positive side of the ledger on climate risk reporting.[24]

With the right execution, this plan would benefit both developed-world corporations *and* burgeoning businesses in developing countries. It is only a germ of an idea, but if you've read this far, you're probably ready to think out of the box. Here goes.

How Green Tax Incentives Would Work

Dozens of consumer goods companies and retailers have together spent billions of dollars designing, developing and purchasing new point-of-sale equipment, air conditioning and refrigeration systems that use natural refrigerants. These new machines eliminate hydrofluorocarbons, one of the super-greenhouse gases that are up to 4,500 times more potent than carbon dioxide. HFCs are becoming so ubiquitous, they could erase all of the climate benefits of the Montreal Protocol if the developing world uses them to cool their new buildings, homes, refrigerators, cars and supermarkets (see chapter 4).

These new non-HFC machines and coolers also provide anywhere from 10 to 50 percent energy savings to their users. Eliminating HFCs and decreasing energy usage are both imperative. Consumer brand giants, such as Coca-Cola, PepsiCo, and

Unilever, have spent tens of millions of dollars developing and deploying these new technologies, but it's their retail customers and other public buildings and institutions that collect the savings on the lower electric bills.

In developing countries, the hardest part for big companies looking to change cooling systems is the creation of a service and maintenance infrastructure (training service personnel with local companies and ensuring available replacement parts). In fact, the major impediment to transforming entire fleets of vending machines and coolers over to non-HFC natural refrigerants is the cost of building this infrastructure.

Yet dozens of corporations have already eliminated a significant amount of greenhouse gas usage and emissions via this refrigeration technology changeover. They could be given special tax credits and incentives for this work anywhere and everywhere. These could take the form of accelerated depreciation allowances, tax credits for greenhouse gas elimination (it is measurable), double or triple credits for clean tech R&D and other special dispensations. All these accounting practices would lower the cost of capital investments to companies. Just as the government encourages homeownership by offering a mortgage tax credit, the government could incentivize companies to invest in green technology. If there were a price on carbon, this transformation would translate to immediate competitive cost advantages. That's why we need a global climate treaty; this treaty will *never* be passed without some tech transfer funding stipulations.

But for creating the expensive service and maintenance infrastructure in the developing world, these American, European or Japanese companies would have real incentives to deploy only state-of-the-art equipment. The rapid creation of this infrastructure would ensure that natural refrigerants are the predominant technology adopted in places just starting to use any commercial refrigeration. Tax incentives can help facilitate this important step.

NO MAINTENANCE INFRASTRUCTURE,
NO NEW TECHNOLOGY

In exchange for these tax savings, these companies would be required to work in partnership with local companies, developing the local service and maintenance infrastructure needed for technological progress on the ground.

This tax saving and extra clean tech investment would then become part of the developed world tech transfer funding commitment.

This idea would require some of major players to seriously shift their thinking, but it also promises them some big opportunities. The U.S. State Department is part of a multinational group advocating for the phase-out of HFCs and other short-acting super-greenhouse gases. Green tax incentives that also serve as foreign policy tools are one way to connect this initiative to the larger climate negotiations.

Conclusion

In the twentieth century, new business practices and advances in science and technology radically transformed the world in which we live, for better and for worse. In addition to providing unbelievably improved health and welfare conditions for over a billion of the world's people, our way of life also caused a dire global environmental crisis.

These innovations are just a few of the many that are in the garage and the laboratory and at the negotiating tables of both companies and countries. They adhere to the NMB Framework, but now it's time for your ideas. The next chapter outlines a path forward, but mostly there is a strong multimedia domain being built for your ideas.

The work will occur in both virtual and real forums called A Transition Agenda, galvanizing participation from the broadest cross section possible. Chapter 8 is an invitation for all readers to join in building a new framework for twenty-first-century commerce. A Transition Agenda will aim to build solutions that address both financial and environmental problems.

OK, let's go.

8

WHY DON'T WE?

A TRANSITION AGENDA

[T]he word of the Lorax seems perfectly clear. UNLESS someone like you cares a whole awful lot, nothing is going to get better. It's not.

—Dr. Seuss (Theodor Seuss Geisel), *The Lorax*

Why Don't They?

Eliminate these three words from your vocabulary.

Instead, get thee to www.transitionagenda.org, where you can collaborate with others to help solve some big problems. Nature and its powerful forces will likely limit and govern our choices in the very near term. So while there is still the possibility of thinking rationally about our circumstances, why don't we?

There are many ways to change the world. Sometimes it involves taking to the streets, sometimes it's working in the weeds and sometimes it is becoming a revolutionary in a suit (whatever suit you happen to wear). In order to change the rules of business and finance, all of us, with our various skill sets and levels of influence (high and low), must become activists.

Your political stripes mean nothing if your food/water/energy supplies are threatened. The only option is for *us* to change the public conversation so that we connect our financial and environmental decisions—in the public, private and individual sectors. This would be a huge shift in the personal, business and political zeitgeist.

When your friends, family, neighbors, politicians and colleagues demonstrate courage and consideration, it becomes the norm. I am a great believer in the importance of cultural context. That goes for your high school, your business, your church, your government, your poker game or Little League. Culture informs both how we make decisions and where we land in those choices. But money talks. My greatest hope is that *Environmental Debt* promulgates new ideas into the culture that in turn change our understanding of business.

I believe that the first fundamental guidelines to move our economy to a sustainable path are those in the Nature Means Business (NMB) Framework. I'm sure you will add others.

1. Pollution can no longer be free and can no longer be subsidized.
2. The long view must guide all decision making and accounting.
3. Government plays a vital role in catalyzing clean technology and growth while preventing environmental destruction.

But getting there is the hard part. We need a transition agenda. Thousands of civil society organizations (health, economic development, human rights and environmental groups), companies and even governments are working to implement all or part of these goals. But very few are addressing financial and environmental problems as a unit, even though they're inextricably linked.

Obviously, policymakers and businesspeople cannot separate business from the world it inhabits, and we cannot address huge public spending deficits when ever-larger environmental debts continue to pile up. But that is our current structure.

The crux of the difficulty becomes clear when you ask the following two questions:

1. If coal and oil cost their true prices based on new financial rules, how will that melt down the economy?
2. If coal and oil continue to be underpriced, how will that melt down the environment?

An extreme weather event like Hurricane Sandy melts down both.

These questions are impossible to unravel and answer without the involvement of a full spectrum of stakeholders. A Transition Agenda will invite disparate groups and the interested public (you) to help chart a course that lowers environmental debt drastically while protecting economic stability. To be clear, when I say "economic stability," I do not mean business as usual. I mean protecting as many businesses and workers and communities as possible during a tumultuous time and providing a real transition for others. I mean changing expectations about what is financially viable and reasonable.

We must be willing to imagine that coal and oil can become minor pieces of the world's economy through a radical reconfiguration of energy, manufacturing and transportation systems. Within two generations, they would be used only when other options are truly not feasible and as bridge fuels to non-fossil fuel energy systems. Getting there will be one helluva journey. But many businesses and scientists believe that it is possible. There is no other alternative if we are to stabilize the world's weather systems for the second half of the twenty-first century and beyond.

The new rules being proposed by those heroic accountants of chapter 3 will come to pass only if an active, engaged public understands their world-changing ideas. We need to advocate for governments to enact these rules rapidly because many businesses and their powerful lobbies are already moving to quash or delay them. But as you've read throughout this book, *many* businesses, including some of the world's largest and best known, are working with these accountants and pushing for the strongest possible changes. I have been amazed at the strange bedfellows in these efforts. It is a genuinely exciting moment.

Meanwhile, many phenomenal technologies and systems are just coming to market or in development for water and energy efficiency. They will be deployed rapidly and at full scale only when their competitors no longer receive a financial advantage by overusing and polluting these same natural resources with no financial penalty. That means that we, the public, might have to spend more in the short term to provide these first movers a strong market advantage. Think of how the expensive organic food market has grown in recent years and imagine that price differential across your entire budget. This would feel very expensive—but not as expensive as building levees to protect all of the population centers on the eastern seaboard of North America. This kind of long-term budgeting is *not* how we are accustomed to counting our money—not in the public, private or individual sectors.

YES, NATURE MEANS BUSINESS

Only when more of us better understand the role of government in the food/water/energy nexus will governments offer incentives and support for green innovation instead of antiquated subsidies that increase environmental debt. Equally important, we must demand that government reduce this irreconcilable debt. This means correcting its omission in every media statement, statistical analysis or annual report. We must always ask, what is the real cost of

The Breezy Point section of Queens, New York after Hurricane Sandy.

Photo by Tim Aubrey, Greenpeace

x? What are the long-term consequences? Government spending is radically increased by environmental debt. So is business's.

The return on investment of business must become intrinsically tied to the survival of the natural world. Eliminating huge amounts of environmental debt from our financial transactions can happen only when we all cooperate on what we produce, what we buy and how we use and dispose of it.

Step One

In my work with corporations and as an environmental activist over many years, the hardest piece of any solution is usually figuring out the first step. It always entails some risk and, often, more time, money and energy than expected. And the second hardest piece of most solutions is figuring out how to scale up a great idea so it becomes normal market activity, technology and behavior.

As I've shown, there are corporations, many of them—and surprising ones—that are already taking first steps and are moving deeply into fundamental change. But with the occasional exception of the European Union (and a few of its member countries) and perhaps California, virtually no governments are willing to join them there. Little surprise. Under no circumstances are the necessary changes politically expedient.

A Transition Agenda is designed for the overwhelming nature of these problems, to concentrate on both big-vision and quick, immediate changes that lay the groundwork for bigger action down the road.

It will serve as your place to construct the addendum to this book. It is your place to become a revolutionary in a suit or a uniform or an apron, with a caulking gun, water collector, petition or surge protector. We'll start with identifying a few work streams for connecting financial and environmental actions and issues. I hope that, within a year, you will have added problems and solutions that large numbers of you want to address. Civil society groups, businesses and government agencies will be invited to partake, lead and follow.

Why Don't We?

Your participation in defining business in the twenty-first century is crucial.

I have partnered with RESOLVE, a Washington, DC–based nonprofit organization. RESOLVE specializes in bringing together people, businesses, civil society organizations and governments that seriously disagree with each other into a solution-building mode. It is now led by Steve D'Esposito, who led Earthworks when it worked with Tiffany & Co. as described in chapter 4.

RESOLVE was created over thirty years ago to bring conflict resolution and a focus on negotiated solutions into the sphere of environmental and public policy. You probably haven't heard of RESOLVE for the simple reason that it succeeds by letting the negotiating partners at the table take the credit for its achievements.

This invisible strength is why the U.S. government called on RESOLVE to negotiate the no-net-loss-of-wetlands rule (a U.S. government policy to balance economic development with wetlands reclamation, mitigation and restoration efforts); why the World Wildlife Fund and Unilever brought it in to guide the development of the Marine Stewardship Council (a global organization to design and implement sustainable fishing practices); and why, in 2012, RESOLVE is working with Intel, Hewlett-Packard and human rights groups to craft solutions to the challenge of "conflict minerals."[1] All of these environmental and social game changers happened because RESOLVE brought disparate ideas and perspectives to coalesce into a solution.

A Transition Agenda needs this kind of leadership to guide the crowdsourcing of ideas and actions through uncharted terrain. And RESOLVE will ensure that those who seriously disagree with me (and maybe you) are at the table. Sometimes this work will happen online and sometimes in face-to-face meetings and conferences.

RESOLVE will lay out the current state of affairs in a few arenas. The website will display the initiatives in the public, private and individual sectors. There will be places to bone up on new information and link to current initiatives. At first, you will be asked only to join and support ongoing initiatives. RESOLVE will work with many civil society groups to open up work streams for readers. Your brains and your brawn will be called on. But you may also decide to launch a new initiative or make connections between initiatives in different sectors. This is how the community grows.

Let's start with the basics: food, water and energy.

Numerous reports have been written on the long-term policy reforms needed in each of these areas. These reports come from organizations and experts from various political and ideological perspectives. But our task is not to write another policy tome. Instead, for each of these issues, we'll simply ask this: With regard to a Transition Agenda, what are some catalyzing actions where the public, private and individual sectors can incorporate the three NMB principles into the economic foundations of food, water and energy? We'll ask many sectors what an engaged public can do to leverage skills and energy to make change.

The work stream will envision long-term policy overhaul but also include a catalyzing action or campaign that can be implemented within three years. For example, as we pursue a total rework of U.S. energy policy, the individual sector might coalesce around voluntarily lowering energy usage by 20 percent. That alone will inexorably alter the financial equations of the energy business. (Lowering the demand changes the economics of creating the supply.) That effort would include utilities, governments, schools, businesses of every kind including energy companies, many civil society groups and public institutions. RESOLVE will connect to those groups already tilling these fields and open the doors for your efforts to augment them.

Very large companies have already used this approach successfully. Procter & Gamble and Unilever both asked the public to weigh in with innovations that would help achieve sustainability goals, and both received highly valuable outside ideas, financial *and* technological. Questions on the companies' open innovation sites ranged from food preservation to detergent composition. And many of us have donated to a project through Kickstarter that bubbled up through our social networks. A Transition Agenda asks for your time and ingenuity. RESOLVE will invite donors and investors to be ready with seed money or start-up capital for ideas generated.

Via the website's platform, you can bring your ideas into the mainstream and work with others to organize the individual sector into a giant conservation and efficiency machine. Or you can seek help from businesses or investors to bring your idea (or others') from the garage to prototype development. Or you can find others to determine if your statistical hunches have merit and turn these analyses into peer-reviewed reports that measure the real costs of a piece of the food/water/energy system.

Each of the projects you create will go through a conceptual phase, where RESOLVE will bring in experts to debate and refine the options through a series of facilitated discussions, some virtual, some in person. Then projects will be shared and tested virally through a curated crowdsourcing process. Organizations, companies and government agencies already in this space will be included in these expert groups. There is no need to reinvent the wheel where great work already is under way. But it is likely that new connections will be made so that an influx of new ideas and energy invigorates work across multiple sectors.

After this vetting, RESOLVE will bring stakeholders across a project's scope (public, private, individual, civil society) to a negotiating table to design a program and plan of action. Depending on your profile, you might be a stakeholder in any of the sectors. Experts will join these discussions at all points of entry.

RESOLVE will then bring in funders/investors/businesses to provide resources to launch these collaborative projects. This is how you will write the addendum to this book.

The NMB Framework is meant to facilitate the move from problems to solutions while acknowledging that the transition will be messy and difficult. We can learn from experience. Think about the revolutionaries in suits I have profiled throughout the book—corporate employees, engineers, accountants, scientists, technocrats, politicians and civil society leaders who demanded all kinds of change. Each embraced a period of uncertainty and experimentation and took a calculated risk to tackle business, social and environmental challenges. We need to do the same.

> The things that will destroy America are prosperity-at-any-price, peace-at-any-price, safety-first instead of duty-first, the love of soft living, and the get-rich-quick theory of life.
>
> —Theodore Roosevelt

At the suggestion of a friend who works at the American Museum of Natural History, I started reading up on Theodore Roosevelt. In the hundred-plus years since Teddy Roosevelt led the nation with his great conservation and wilderness initiatives, the natural landscape and wilderness have been enormously degraded. However, protecting and loving the land can reenter our lexicon, cultural perspective and economic purview if enough of us exercise these values in our decision making. This is a *pro*-business sentiment—pro-*long-term* business.

Why don't we?

As Theodore Roosevelt warned, the desire for fast, cheap and convenient has overtaken most other values where culture meets commerce. Today's culture rewards and exalts short-term pleasure, easy access and personal aggrandizement above most everything else. And business rules currently provide this way of life for corporations as well as their customers. How do we change that? Some of it is economics, some of it is policy and some of it is individual actions. But one thing's for sure: This would be a fundamental cultural shift.

The days after the September 11 attacks were an awful time in New York, for reasons I do not need to explain. But it was also a time full of grace. Everyone who visited here could feel this palpably. Anyone, everyone, in every business, school, hospital, grocery, subway and sidewalk, *everywhere*. There was a feeling that one wanted to take care of the people and the place around you because there was such a clear sense of the fragility and insecurity of everything. This lasted about two months, but everyone here remembers and still talks about it. Our very membranes had been attacked, and we all wished to be our greatest selves.

We are now in an era of enormous instability—environmentally, politically and economically. Actually, 2012's extreme weather may have already altered our perception of predictability and security where weather is concerned. And if we followed the environmental news as closely as we follow the stock market, we would see that the planet's environmental stability is under siege. This shift in perception and priorities has got to last more than two months.

This is our chance to create a new paradigm, where we use Earth's resources more wisely, make money more responsibly, spend money on products that last and do not cause lasting damage and treat energy and water as the precious and finite resources they are.

This is how we will connect the globalized economic system to the global ecosystem.

Nothing except nature can transform the world as swiftly as can business—for better or for worse.

When Lyndon Johnson signed the Voting Rights Act in 1965, he had a country trembling with demonstrators who demanded their civil rights. When Ed Muskie and Howard Baker led the fight for the first Clean Air Act in 1970, they each credited the broad environmental movement, newly embodied by Earth Day, as their backup. When Candy Lightner's thirteen-year-old daughter was killed by a drunken driver in 1980, she channeled her grief and rage into the founding of Mothers Against Drunk Driving (MADD). And when Democratic governor Andrew Cuomo of New York State signed the Marriage Equality Act in 2011, he and

THIS LAND IS YOUR LAND

Words and Music by Woody Guthrie

This land is your land
This land is my land
From California to the New York island;
From the red wood forest to the Gulf Stream waters
This land was made for you and me.

As I was walking that ribbon of highway,
I saw above me that endless skyway:
I saw below me that golden valley:
This land was made for you and me.
I've roamed and rambled and I followed my footsteps To the
    sparkling sands of her diamond deserts;
And all around me a voice was sounding:
This land was made for you and me.

the bill's Republican sponsors cited the millions of gay people and their friends and families who had spent decades bringing sexual equality into the mainstream through large-scale protests as well as intimate family gatherings.

And now we must connect our financial and environmental nervous systems. In the last few decades, modern medicine has helped us to understand that our minds and bodies are not separate and, as a rule, must be treated together. The same now goes for our financial and environmental systems. We cannot address the causes and solutions of financial debt without including environmental debt in all of our calculations. They are one unit.

Today, wherever you are, there is a sense that the ground is moving, both financially and environmentally. We need to reboot a crashing system. There is a real hunger to build a foundation so that the twenty-first century doesn't feel so bloody scary. Look around your office, your home, your school, your government. We are all facing very difficult choices. It is time to work together.

Why don't we?

ACKNOWLEDGMENTS

So many people helped me with this book. It is a veritable treasure trove of intelligence, insight and support. A few people were essential ingredients—Kimbell Duncan, Kjris Lund, Catherine Babcock, Lisa Finaldi, Cynthia Scharf, and Kay Treakle. Steve D'Esposito provided insight and support at crucial times. And Gary Stewart, Marina Galanti, Joe Lertola, Amy Solomon, Doug Koplow, Mary Hadar, Harry Lodge, Janet Ginsburg, Molly Dorozenski, Kelly Rigg and Stan McBarnette all stepped in regularly. Charlie Cray, Mark Floegel, Mike Johnson, Jim Riccio and Keith Nowak all provided useful information. Ray Mendez and Concept Farm keep me in crazy ideas and happy office space. And Anastasi Siotas and Phyllis Cohen help with just about everything.

Johanna Goetzel, in addition to being a main researcher, also served as my first set of eyes and often helped me clarify my thoughts. This was a tremendous gift.

Greg Larkin and Diana Propper were my B.S. barometers, and Pauline Larkin, Rhea Leman and Susan Friedman were touchstones throughout. James and Mary Larkin also provided support early and often.

Many of my Greenpeace friends and colleagues have inspired me over so many years, but a special shout-out to Kert Davies,

Paula Tejon, Sultan Latif, Claudette Pappas, Janos Mate and Wolo Lohbeck. I would wish a team like this on every difficult endeavor and a set of friends like this for anyone in good times and bad.

My agent Laura Yorke helped me sculpt this book. Her commentary was always demanding and always helpful. And somehow she made me laugh hysterically while grilling me with more demands. And special thanks to Antonia Bowring for introducing us.

From the minute I met my editor, Emily Carleton, I knew she was serious about bringing these ideas to the public. And she has proven me right.

But most of all, I tip my hat to the dozens of revolutionaries in corporate suits with whom I collaborated while at Greenpeace. They restored my faith that a few well-meaning people who disagree on many, many things can still listen to each other and work together to achieve dramatic results. We need more of them!

APPENDIX TO CHAPTER 5

Some of the categories used in the next tables sound impersonal. "Mortality and morbidity" means a miner in West Virginia died from coal dust at age forty-five and left a family in a terrible state. "Developmental disabilities" from mercury poisoning caused by coal combustion means a child cannot process or function well, a family has to tend to the child and a school system has to educate this low-functioning child. This is devastating for a family—especially one with low or moderate income. "Workplace fatalities and injuries" are the images we have all seen on the news of miners in deadly accidents. The Harvard report shines a light on costs, but the real impacts on real people is what should move us to change. (MTR stands for mountaintop removal—the practice of blowing off the top of a mountain to build a mine.)

Sector/Area	Economic Impacts	Human Health	Environment	Other
Underground coal mining	Federal and state subsidies of coal industry	Increased mortality and morbidity in coal communities due to mining pollution Threats remaining from abandoned mine lands	Methane emissions from coal leading to climate change Remaining damage from abandoned mine lands	
MTR mining	Tourism loss Significantly lower property values Cost to taxpayers of environmental mitigation and monitoring (both mining and disposal stages)	Contaminated streams Direct trauma in surrounding communities Additional mortality and morbidity in coal communities due to increased levels of air particulates associated with MTR mining (vs. underground mining)	Loss of biodiversity Sludge and slurry Greater levels of air particulate Loss and contamination of streams	
Coal Combustion	Federal and state subsidies for the coal industry Damage to farmland and crops resulting from coal combustion pollution	Increased mortality and morbidity due to combustion pollution acid rain Hospitalization costs resulting from increased morbidity in coal communities Higher frequency of sudden infant death syndrome in areas with high quantities of particulate pollution	Climate change due to CO and NO_x derived N_2O emissions Environmental contamination as a result of heavy metal pollution (mercury, selenium, arsenic) Impacts of acid rain derived from nitrogen oxides and SO_2 Environmental impacts of ozone and particulate emissions Soil contamination from acid rain Destruction of marine life from mercury pollution and acid rain Freshwater use in coal powered plants	Corrosion of buildings and monuments from acid rain Visibility impairment from NO_x emissions

Sector/Area	Economic Impacts	Human Health	Environment	Other
Coal Mining	Opportunity costs of bypassing other types of economic development (especially for MTR mining) Infrastructure damage due to mudslides following MTR Federal and state subsidies of coal industry Economic boom and bust cycle in coal mining communities Cost of coal industry litigation Damage to farmland and crops resulting from coal mining pollution Loss of income from small-scale forest gathering and farming (e.g., wild ginseng, mushrooms) due to habitat loss Loss of tourism income Lower property values for homeowners	Workplace fatalities and injuries of coal miners Morbidity and mortality of mine workers resulting from air pollution (e.g., black lung, silicosis) Increased mortality and morbidity in coal communities due to mining pollution Increased morbidity and mortality due to increased air particulates in communities proximate to MTR mining Hospitalization costs resulting from increased morbidity in coal communities Population losses in abandoned coal-mining communities Local health impacts of heavy metals in coal slurry Mental and dental health impacts reported, possibly from heavy metals	Destruction of local habitat and biodiversity to develop mine site Infrastructure damage due to mudslides following MTR Methane emissions from coal leading to climate change Damage to surrounding infrastructure from subsidence Loss of habitat and streams from valley fill (MTR) Damages to buildings and other infrastructure due to mine blasting Loss of recreation availability in coal mining communities Incomplete reclamation following mine use Water pollution from runoff and waste spills Air pollution due to increased particulates from MTR mining Remaining damage from abandoned mine lands	Infrastructure damage due to mudslides following MTR Damage to surrounding infrastructure from subsidence Damages to buildings and other infrastructure due to mine blasting Loss of recreation availability in coal mining communities Population losses in abandoned coal-mining communities

Sector/Area	Economic Impacts	Human Health	Environment	Other
Coal Transportation	Wear and tear on aging railroads and tracks Federal and state subsidies for the coal industry	Death and injuries from accidents during transport Increased mortality and morbidity due to combustion pollution	Impacts from emissions during transport Damage to vegetation resulting from air pollution	Damage to rail system from coal transportation Damage to roadways due to coal trucks
Waste Disposal		Health impacts of heavy metals and other contaminants in coal ash and other waste Health impacts, trauma and loss of property following coal ash spills	Water pollution from runoff and fly ash spills Impacts on surrounding ecosystems from coal ash and other waste	
Electricity Transmission	Loss of energy in the combustion and transmission phases		Disturbance of ecosystems by utility towers and rights of way	Vulnerability of electrical grid to climate change associated disasters

Plant Type	Capacity Factor (%)	U.S. Average Levelized Cost for Plants Entering Service in 2017 (2010 USD/MWh)				
		Levelized Capital Cost	Fixed O&M	Variable O&M (including fuel)	Transmission Investment	Total System Levelized Cost
Conventional Coal	85	65.8	4.0	28.6	1.2	99.6
Advanced Coal	85	75.2	6.6	29.2	1.2	112.2
Advanced Coal with CCS	85	93.3	9.3	36.8	1.2	140.7
Natural Gas Fired						
Conventional Combined Cycle	87	17.5	1.9	48.0	1.2	68.6
Advanced Combined Cycle	87	17.9	1.9	44.4	1.2	65.5
Advanced CC with CCS	87	34.9	4.0	52.7	1.2	92.8

Source: U.S. Energy Information Administration

Plant Type	Capacity Factor (%)	U.S. Average Levelized Cost for Plants Entering Service in 2017 (2010 USD/MWh)				
		Levelized Capital Cost	Fixed O&M	Variable O&M (including fuel)	Transmission Investment	Total System Levelized Cost
Conventional Combustion Turbine	30	46.0	2.7	79.9	3.6	132.0
Advanced Combustion Turbine	30	31.7	2.6	67.5	3.6	105.3
Advanced Nuclear	90	88.8	11.3	11.6	1.1	112.7
Geothermal	92	76.6	11.9	9.6	1.5	99.6
Biomass	83	56.8	13.8	48.3	1.3	120.2
Wind[1]	34	83.3	9.7	0.0	3.7	96.8
Wind — Offshore[1]	27	300.6	22.4	0.0	7.7	330.6
Solar PV[1,2]	25	144.9	7.7	0.0	4.2	156.9

Source: U.S. Energy Information Administration

NOTES

1 A FRAMEWORK FOR TWENTY-FIRST-CENTURY COMMERCE

1. "Commodities Rise to Two-Year High as Cotton Jumps to Record, Cocoa Gains," *Cotton Market News,* March 4, 2011, http://cotton marketnews.com/2012/09/17/world-cotton-output-forecast-at-114mn -bales-in-201213/ and http://www.indexmundi.com/commodities/?commo dity=soybeans.
2. "Good Year for Farmers Making Solar Power," CBC News, August 13, 2012, http://www.cbc.ca/news/technology/story/2012/08/12/ottawa-solar -power-farmer-good-year.html.
3. K. L. Bassil, "Cancer Health Effects of Pesticides; Systematic Review," *Canadian Family Physician,* October 2007, http://www.cfp.ca/content/53/10 /1704.full.
4. Nelson D. Schwartz and Susanne Craig, "This Bonus Season on Wall Street, Many See Zeros," *New York Times,* December 19, 2010, http://www .nytimes.com/2010/12/20/business/20bonus.html?pagewanted=all&_r=0.
5. Lucas Mearian, "Thai Floods Catapult Seagate into Hard Drive Market Lead," *Computer World,* February 29, 2012, http://www.computer world.com/s/article/9224778/Thai_floods_catapult_Seagate_into_hard _drive_market_lead.
6. Anna Mukai and Yuki Hagiwara, "Toyota Cuts Annual Profit Forecast by 54% After Thai Floods Disrupt Output," Bloomberg, December 9, 2011, http://www.bloomberg.com/news/2011-12-09/toyota-cuts-annual-profit -forecast-by-54-after-thai-floods-disrupt-output.html.
7. "Triclosan Facts," United States Environmental Protection Agency, http:// www.epa.gov/oppsrrd1/REDs/factsheets/triclosan_fs.htm#summary.
8. "Triclosan (Endocrine Disruptor)," Food and Water Watch, http://www .foodandwaterwatch.org/water/triclosan/.
9. "Activist Group Wants Ban on Triclosan, Chemical Found in Personal Care Products," *Global News,* http://www.globalnews.ca/activist+group +wants+ban+on+triclosan+chemical+found+in+personal+care+products /6442642877/story.html.
10. "High-Performance Computing Act of 1991," Networking and Information Technology Research and Development (NITRD), http://www.nitrd .gov/Congressional/Laws/pl_102-194.aspx.

11. Keith Perine, "The Early Adopter—Al Gore and the Internet—Government Activity," *The Industry Standard,* October 10, 2000.

2 ENVIRONMENTAL DEBT

1. "Water," World Economic Forum, http://www.weforum.org/issues/water.
2. "The Truth about Green Jobs (A Case Study)," Center for American Progress, http://www.americanprogress.org/issues/green/news/2012/04/24/11419/the-truth-about-green-jobs-a-case-study/.
3. "Jobs in Renewable Energy Expanding," WorldWatch Institute, http://www.worldwatch.org/node/5821.
4. John Lippert and Jim Efstathiou Jr., "Las Vegas Running Out of Water Means Dimming Los Angeles Lights," Bloomberg, February 26, 2009, http://www.bloomberg.com/apps/news?pid=newsarchive&sid=a_b86mnWn9.w.
5. "Yuba County Agencies Expect to Shake Federal Voting Rights Act Oversight," Aquafornia, http://www.aquafornia.com/index.php/category/water-agency-news/.
6. James Hansen, "Game Over for the Climate," *New York Times,* May 9, 2012, http://www.nytimes.com/2012/05/10/opinion/game-over-for-the-climate.html?_r=1&pagewanted=all.
7. "Canadian Oil Sands," American Petroleum Institute, May 2011, http://www.google.com/url?sa=t&rct=j&q=&esrc=s&source=web&cd=1&ved=0CDwQFjAA&url=http%3A%2F%2Fwww.api.org%2F~%2Fmedia%2FFiles%2FOil-and-Natural-Gas%2FOil_Sands%2FOIL_SANDS_PRIMER_MAY_2011.pdf&ei=jh-hUJGaMo6E0QGvrICgDA&usg=AFQjCNHA4-G5t7-T00cUUnr9CR9GmKA7sw.
8. "Cost of War," http://costofwar.com/; Steve Hargreaves, "A $2 Trillion Bet on Powering America," CNN Money, January 6, 2009, http://money.cnn.com/2009/01/06/news/economy/smart_grid/index.htm.
9. William Anderegg et al., "Expert Credibility in Climate Change," *Proceedings of the National Academy of Sciences in the United States of America* (PNAS), April 2012, http://www.pnas.org/content/107/27/12107.
10. David A. Fahrenthold, "Apple Leaves U.S. Chamber over Its Climate Position," *Washington Post,* October 6, 2009, www.washingtonpost.com/wp-dyn/content/article/2009/10/05/AR2009100502744.html.
11. Richard T. Griffiths, "Climate Change Compounds Global Security Threat, British Admiral Says," September 28, 2011, http://security.blogs.cnn.com/2011/09/28/climate-change-compounds-global-security-threat-british-admiral-says/.
12. The July 16, 1975 issue of the trade magazine *Chemical Weekly* quoting the chair of the board of DuPont, manufacturer of ozone-depleting compounds.
13. "The State of American Business 2010," address by Thomas J. Donohue, president and CEO, U.S. Chamber of Commerce, January 12, 2010, http://www.uschamber.com/press/speeches/2010/state-american-business-2010-address-thomas-j-donohue-president-and-ceo-us-chamb.
14. In a letter to the editor of the *Charleston (WV) Gazette,* dated October 30, 2009.
15. Paul Polman, CEO of Unilever, as quoted at GreenBiz.com SmartBrief on Sustainability on August 20, 2012.

16. Matthew L. Wald, "Offshore Wind Power Line Wins Backing," *New York Times,* October 12, 2010, http://www.nytimes.com/2010/10/12/science /earth/12wind.html?pagewanted=all&_r=0.
17. "Data Centers and Renewable Energy," Apple and the Environment, http://www.apple.com/environment/renewable-energy/.
18. Chloe Albanesius, "How Much Electricity Does Google Consume Each Year?" *PC Mag,* September 8, 2011, http://www.pcmag.com/article2/0,281 7,2392654,00.asp.

3 THE QUEST FOR TRUE PROFITS

1. "PUMA and PPR HOME Announce First Results of Unprecedented Environmental Profit & Loss Account," Puma.com, May 16, 2011, http://about.puma.com/puma-and-ppr-home-announce-first-results-of-unprece dented-environmental-profit-loss-account/.
2. "KPMG Report—Accounting and Financial Reporting Quarterly Update," KPMG, December 2012, http://www.kpmg.com/us/en/issuesandinsights /articlespublications/taxnewsflash/pages/accounting-financial-reporting -quarterly-update-december-2012.aspx.
3. United Nations Environment Programme, http://www.unep.org/.
4. Pavan Sukhdev, "Putting a Price on Nature: The Economics of Ecosystems and Biodiversity," *Solutions Journal,* Volume 1, Issue 6, January 2011, 34-43, http://www.thesolutionsjournal.com/node/823.
5. "100% Recycled Bathroom Tissue," Seventh Generation, www.seventh generation.com/Recycled-Toilet-Paper.
6. "Report of the United Nations Conference on Environment and Development," Rio de Janeiro, June 3-14, 1992, http://www.un.org/documents/ga /conf151/aconf15126-1annex1.htm
7. Ben Geman, "Head of GOP Solyndra Probe Rebuffs Push for Nuke Loan Inquiry," The Hill, February 16, 2012, http://thehill.com/blogs/e2-wire /e2-wire/211127-head-of-gop-solyndra-probe-rebuffs-push-for-nuke-loan -inquiry.
8. "U.S. Solar Industry Grew by 109% in 2011," Solar Tribune, March 16, 2012, http://solartribune.com/report-u-s-solar-industry-grew-by-109-in-2011/.
9. "Campaign by Fidelity," see website and YouTube videos. Print ad found in *Boston Business Journal,* http://thinkingbig.fidelity.com/?ccsource=You Tube&vsheadline=thinking_big&vssource=landing_zone; Lisa van der Pool, "Fidelity Tries Its Hand at Viral Advertising," *Boston Business Journal,* February 27, 2012, www.bizjournals.com/boston/news/2012/02/27 /fidelity-hopes-new-ad-push-will-go-viral.html?page=all.
10. "Beating the Coming Water Shortage," CNN Money, October 12, 2011, http://money.cnn.com/galleries/2011/technology/1110/gallery.water_short age_solutions.fortune/7.html.
11. "World Charter for Nature," U.N. General Assembly, October 28, 1982, http://www.un.org/documents/ga/res/37/a37r007.htm.
12. N. Stern, "Stern Review on The Economics of Climate Change" (pre-publication edition), Executive Summary (London: HM Treasury, London).
13. Alison Benjamin, "Stern: Climate Change a 'Market Failure,'" *The Guardian,* November 29, 2007, http://www.guardian.co.uk/environment/2007 /nov/29/climatechange.carbonemissions.

14. Pavan Sukhdev, "The Economics of Ecosystems and Biodiversity," Bridging the Gap, www.bridgingthegap.si/pdf/Biodiversity%20and%20ecosystems /Pavan%20Sukhdev%20THE%20ECONOMICS%20OF%20ECOSYS TEMS%20AND%20BIODIVERSITY.pdf.

15. Denis Holmark et al., *The Annual Environmental Report: Measuring and Reporting Environmental Performance* (Copenhagen: Price Waterhouse, 1995).

16. R. G. Eccles, M. Krzus, *One Report: Integrated Reporting for a Sustainable Strategy* (New Jersey: Wiley, 2010), http://www.amazon.com/One -Report-Integrated-Reporting-Eccles-M-Krzus/dp/B003PJ8SAM.

17. Global Reporting Initiative, https://www.globalreporting.org/.

18. International Organization for Standardization, http://www.iso.org/iso /home.html.

19. Integrated Reporting, http://www.theiirc.org/.

20. "SEC Issues Interpretive Guidance on Disclosure Related to Business or Legal Developments Regarding Climate Change," U.S. Securities and Exchange Commission, January 27, 2010, www.sec.gov/news/press/2010/2010-15 .htm.

4 COURAGE

1. Union of Concerned Scientists, www.ucsusa.org/, and analysis from the Council on Foreign Relations, http://www.cfr.org/natural-resources-manage ment/deforestation-greenhouse-gas-emissions/p14919.

2. "Eating up the Amazon," April 6, 2006, http://www.greenpeace.org.uk /media/reports/eating-up-the-amazon.

3. "Cargill's View on the Greenpeace Report: Eating Up the Amazon," Cargill, May 2006, www.brazilink.org/tiki-download_file.php?fileId=194.

4. The emphasis is McDonald's.

5. "10 Questions: CR Leaders Corner: Bob Langert," Accountability, May 1, 2012, http://www.accountability.org/about-us/news/cr-leaders-corner/bob -langert.html.

6. "The Baia Mare Gold Mine Cyanide Spill: Causes, Impacts and Liability," Relief Web, Greenpeace, April 12, 2000, http://reliefweb.int/report /hungary/baia-mare-gold-mine-cyanide-spill-causes-impacts-and-liability; "Newmont Gold Mine to Pay Ghana Millions for Cyanide Spill," Environment News Service, January 22, 2000, http://www.ens-newswire.com/ens /jan2010/2010-01-22-01.html.

7. "Baia Mare Cyanide Spill," Toxipedia, http://toxipedia.org/display/toxi pedia/Baia+Mare+Cyanide+Spill.

8. "Resource Efficiency," United Nations Environment Programme, http:// www.unep.fr/scp/business/vi/sector/gold.htm.

9. Jared Diamond. *Guns, Germs, and Steel: The Fates of Human Societies* (New York: W. W. Norton, 1997).

10. Maggie Koerth-Baker, "4 Rare Earth Elements That Will Only Get More Important," *Popular Mechanics,* http://www.popularmechanics.com/tech nology/engineering/news/important-rare-earth-elements#slide-1.

11. Simon Sharwood, "Malaysia Protests Rare Earth Processing Plant," November 9, 2012, www.theregister.co.uk/2012/11/09/malaysia_rare_earth _protests_against_lyanas_corp/.

12. "What Are 'Rare Earths' Used For?" BBC News World, March 12, 2012, http://www.bbc.co.uk/news/world-17357863.

13. In 2012, a Montana court finally ruled against the mine's approval.

14. "In Wake of Dispatches Expos, Jewellery Customers Want to Avoid Dirty Gold," Earthworks, June 28, 2011, http://www.earthworksaction.org /media/detail/in_wake_of_dispatches_expos_jewellery_customers_want _to_avoid_dirty_gold.

15. Clifford Kraus, "U.S. Oil and Mining Companies Must Disclose Payments to Foreign Governments," New York Times, August 22, 2012, http://www .nytimes.com/2012/08/23/business/sec-votes-to-require-more-disclosure -on-source-of-minerals.html.

16. "Wal-Mart Chairman: How We Came to Embrace Sustainability," CNN Money, April 17, 2012, http://tech.fortune.cnn.com/2012/04/17 /rob-walton-peter-seligmann-transcript/.

17. Jonathan Rowe, "The Greening of Wal-Mart," American Prospect, April 19, 2011, http://prospect.org/article/greening-wal-mart.

18. "Walmart Eliminates More than 80 Percent of Its Waste in California That Would Otherwise Go to Landfills," Walmart.com, http://news.walmart .com/news-archive/2011/03/17/walmart-eliminates-more-than-80-percent -of-its-waste-in-california-that-would-otherwise-go-to-landfills.

19. "Top 10 Ways Walmart Made a Difference in 2011," Walmart.com, http:// www.walmartstores.com/sites/responsibility-report/2012/top10.aspx.

20. "Two Thought-provoking Perspectives on the 'Crisis of Capitalism,'" First Friday Book Synopsis, http://ffbsccn.wordpress.com/2011/04/05 /two-thought-provoking-perspectives-on-the-crisis-of-capitalism/.

21. "Reducing Deforestation through Sustainable Supply Chains," USAID, June 21, 2012, http://www.usaid.gov/news-information/press-releases /reducing-deforestation-through-sustainable-supply-chains.

22. "Danger in the Air: Unhealthy Air Days in 2010 and 2011," Environment America, September 21, 2011, http://www.environmentamerica.org /reports/ame/danger-air-unhealthy-air-days-2010-and-2011.

23. Lee Iacocca, executive vice president of Ford Motor Company, in 1970, on why the government shouldn't regulate airborne contaminants that are hazardous to human health, from The New Republic, "Women's Suffrage and Other Visions of Right-Wing Apocalypse."

24. "Decision of the Administrator of the Environmental Protection Agency Regarding Suspension of the 1975 Auto Emission Standards, Part 1," Hearings before the Subcommittee on Air and Water Pollution of the Committee on Public Works U.S. Senate 93rd Congress, First session, April 16–18, 1973.

25. "Cleaning America's Air—Progress And Challenges," Muskie Foundation, University of Tennessee, Knoxville, March 9, 2005, http://www.muskie foundation.org/baker.030905.html.

26. "Empirical Evidence Regarding the Effects of the Clean Air Act on Jobs and Economic Growth," Committee of Energy and Commerce, http:// democrats.energycommerce.house.gov/sites/default/files/documents/White Paper_CleanAirAct.pdf.

27. Edmund S. Muskie, "NEPA to CERCLA: The Clear Air Act: A Commitment to Public Health," Clean Air Trust, http://www.cleanairtrust.org /nepa2cercla.html.

28. The July 16, 1975, issue of the trade magazine Chemical Weekly quoted the chair of the board of DuPont saying this.

29. "The Ozone Hole History," The Ozone Hole, http://www.theozonehole .com/ozoneholehistory.htm.

30. After losing $57 billion in weather-related claims between 1990 and 1995, compared to $17 billion for the preceding decade, some insurance companies concluded that increased weather extremes could be devastating. Franklin Nutter, president of the Reinsurance Association of America, summed up the threat. http://www.worldwatch.org/pressure-climate-negotiatiors-heats.

31. T. Barker et al., "Technical Summary," in *Climate Change 2007: Mitigation. Contribution of Working Group III to the Fourth Assessment Report of the Intergovernmental Panel on Climate Change* (Cambridge, United Kingdom: Cambridge University Press), http://www.ipcc.ch/pdf/assessment-report/ar4/wg3/ar4-wg3-ts.pdf.

32. "HFCs and Other F-gases: The Worst Greenhouse Gases You've Never Heard Of," Greenpeace, http://www.greenpeace.org/international/Global /international/planet-2/report/2009/5/HFCs-Fgases.pdf.

33. René van Gerwen, "Ice Cream Cabinets Using Hydrocarbon Refrigerant from Technology Concept to Global Rollout," Unilever.com, http://www .unilever.com/images/Ice%20Cream%20Cabinets%20Using%20a%20 Hydrocarbon%20Refrigerant%20-%20From%20Technology%20Concept %20to%20Global%20Rollout_tcm13-262015.pdf.

5 MOVING BEYOND FOSSIL FUELS

1. "The Operational and Strategic Rationale Behind the U.S. Military's Energy Efforts," Consumer Energy Report, www.consumerenergyreport. com/2012/06/07/the-operational-and-strategic-rationale-behind-the-u-s -militarys-energy-efforts/; "Clean Energy Trends 2012," Clean Edge, http:// www.cleanedge.com/reports/clean-energy-trends-2012.

2. Matt Brian, "Google Continues Renewable Energy Focus with Wind Power Deal for Oklahoma Data Center," The Next Web, http://thenextweb.com /google/2012/09/26/google-continues-renewable-energy-focus-wind -power-deal-oklahoma-data-center/.

3. Mauro Whiteman, "Greenpeace Upgrades Apple on 'Coal-free' Promise," Mediafile, July 12, 2012, http://blogs.reuters.com/mediafile/2012/07/12 /apple-greenpeace-renewable-energy/.

4. "Environment," Corporate Social Responsibility, Cisco, http://csr.cisco .com/pages/environment.

5. Bill Estep, "Coal Industry Sheds Jobs, Leaving Eastern Kentucky Economy in Tatters," McClatchy, July 29, 2012, http://www.mcclatchy dc.com/2012/07/29/158502/coal-industry-sheds-jobs-leaving.html#story link=cpy.

6. Nuclear Engineering International, http://www.neimagazine.com/story.asp ?sectioncode=147&storyCode=2058653.

7. Jeff Himmelman, "The Secret to Solar Power," *New York Times Magazine,* http://www.nytimes.com/2012/08/12/magazine/the-secret-to-solar-power .html?_r=2&pagewanted=all&.

8. "German Solar Power Plants," *YouTube,* https://www.youtube.com/watch ?v=9__6CEveW6k.

9. Barbara Lewis, "EU Wind Capacity Hits 100 Gigawatt Mark—Industry," Reuters, September 27, http://uk.mobile.reuters.com/article/idUKBRE88Q 0K220120927?irpc=932.

10. "The California Solar Initiative—CSI," Go Solar California, http://www .gosolarcalifornia.org/csi/index.php.

11. "National Solar Jobs Census 2011," The Solar Foundation, October 2011, http://www.thesolarfoundation.org/sites/thesolarfoundation.org/files/TSF_JobsCensus2011_Final_Compressed.pdf.

12. Michael Hiltzik, "Has Blazing a Trail in Solar Energy Cost California Too Much?" *Los Angeles Times*, May 23, 2012, http://articles.latimes.com/2012/may/23/business/la-fi-hiltzik-20120523.

13. "California Solar Initiative—Annual Program Assessment," California Public Utilities Commission, June 2012, http://www.cpuc.ca.gov/NR/rdonlyres/0C43123F-5924-4DBE-9AD2-8F07710E3850/0/CASolarInitiativeCSIAnnualProgAssessmtJune2012FINAL.pdf.

14. Pace Now, http://pacenow.org/.

15. Charles Q. Choi, "Solar Power's Greenhouse Emissions Measured," Live Science, February 26, 2008, http://www.livescience.com/2324-solar-power-greenhouse-emissions-measured.html.

16. "Duke Energy Customers Owe $2.5 Billion-plus for Edwardsport Plant," Indystar, December 27, 2012, http://www.indystar.com/article/20121227/BUSINESS/121227022/Duke-Energy-customers-owe-2-5-billion-plus-Edwardsport-plant.

17. "Standby Power," Lawrence Berkeley National Laboratory, http://standby.lbl.gov/faq.html.

18. "Levelized Cost of New Generation Resources in the Annual Energy Outlook 2011," Report of the U.S. Energy Information Administration of the U.S. Department of Energy, January 23, 2012.

19. Julie Wernau, "If Chicago Ditches ComEd, Those Still With Utility Would Pay More Experts," *Chicago Tribune*, June 26, 2012, http://articles.chicagotribune.com/2012-06-26/business/ct-biz-adv-chi-aggregation-201 20626-55_1_comed-alternative-suppliers-electricity-deal.

20. "Inside Lines," PJM, June 2012, http://www.pjm.com/about-pjm/news room/newsletter-notices/inside-lines/2012/june.aspx?p=1.

21. Energy & Environment, Americans for Prosperity Texas, http://americans forprosperity.org/texas/issues/energy-environment/.

22. "National Top 50," EPA, October 4, 2012, http://www.epa.gov/green power/toplists/top50.htm.

23. David Roberts, "Hey, Look, a Republican Who Cares About Climate Change!" Grist, http://grist.org/article/hey-look-a-republican-who-cares-about-climate-change/.

24. UNEP FI Global Roundtable, http://www.unepfi.org/grt/session-speakers-a-l/.

25. According to Pike Research, a part of Navigant's Energy Practice, U.S. military spending on renewable energy programs, including conservation measures, will increase steadily over the next twelve years, reaching almost $1.8 billion in 2025.

26. Diane Cardwell, "Tax Credit in Doubt, Wind Power Industry Is Withering," *New York Times*, September 20, 2012, http://www.nytimes.com/2012/09/21/business/energy-environment/as-a-tax-credit-wanes-jobs-vanish-in-wind-power-industry.html?pagewanted=all&_moc.semityn.www.

27. Samsung press release, http://www.samsungrenewableenergy.ca/response-to-ont-pc-party-release.

28. "Progress Report 2012: Economy," Government of Ontario, http://www.gov.on.ca/en/initiatives/progressreport2012/ONT05_040343.html.

29. "Japan Cabinet Approves Plan to Exit Nuclear Energy," Reuters, September 9, 2012, http://www.reuters.com/article/2012/09/19/us-energy-japan-nuclear-idUSBRE88I05X20120919?feedType=RSS&feedName=environmentNews&utm_source=twitterfeed&utm_medium=twitter&utm_campaign=Feed:+reuters/environment+(News+/+US+/+Environment).

30. George Hohmann, "Trend Forecaster Paints Grim Picture," *Charleston Daily Mail,* March 23, 2011, http://www.dailymail.com/News/201103230062.

31. Guy Chazan, "Total Warns Against Oil Drilling in the Arctic," *Financial Times,* September 25, 2012, http://www.ft.com/cms/s/0/350be724-070a-11e2-92ef-00144feabdc0.html#axzz27Yqfqzxc.

32. Lester Brown, "Considering the Real Costs of Our Energy Economy," *Huffington Post,* January 24, 2007, http://www.huffingtonpost.com/lester-brown/considering-the-real-cost_b_39455.html.

33. Bill Moore, "The Hidden Cost of Our Oil Dependence," EVWorld.com, http://www.evworld.com/syndicated/evworld_article_1018.cfm.

34. Nick Squires, "More Bikes Sold than Cars in Italy for the First Time Since WW2," *The Telegraph,* October 2, 2012, http://www.businessinsider.com/more-bikes-sold-than-cars-in-italy-for-the-first-time-since-ww2-2012-10.

35. Nancy Folbre, "The Bicycle Dividend," Economix blog, *New York Times,* July 4, 2011, http://economix.blogs.nytimes.com/2011/07/04/the-bicycle-dividend/.

36. Jigar Shah, "India's Blackout Exposes Choice Between Water & Electricity," GigaOM, August 2, 2012, http://gigaom.com/cleantech/indias-blackout-exposes-choice-between-water-and-electricity/

37. "Spending on New Renewable Energy Capacity to Total $7 Trillion Over Next 20 Years," Bloomberg New Energy Finance, November 16, 2011, http://bnef.com/PressReleases/view/173.

38. Brad Johnson, "The $20 Trillion Carbon Bubble: Interview with John Fullerton, Part One," Think Progress Climate, March 26, 2012, http://thinkprogress.org/climate/2012/03/26/432617/the-20-trillion-carbon-bubble-interview-with-john-fullerton-part-one/?mobile=nc.

39. Andrew Winston gives thanks to climate überblogger Joe Romm for uncovering this data from the Energy Information Agency in his blog, http://www.bloomberg.com/news/2012-09-26/the-supposed-decline-of-green-energy.html.

40. Samuel Blackstone, "Germany Is Showing the World How to Become a Renewable Energy Powerhouse," Business Insider, July 26, 2012, http://www.businessinsider.com/germany-renewable-energy-production-is-living-up-to-the-hype-2012-7#ixzz2Hrl35UhB.

6 EXTREME WEATHER AND THE FOOD/WATER/ENERGY NEXUS

1. "Nightmare in New York City; Michael Moore Weighs In; Evacuations at NYC Hospitals; Global Warming to Cause More Major Storms?" Transcript, *Piers Morgan Tonight,* October 31, 2012, http://transcripts.cnn.com/TRANSCRIPTS/1210/31/pmt.01.html.

2. "New York City Hurricane Evacuation Zones," *New York Times,* August 26, 2011, http://www.nytimes.com/interactive/2011/08/26/nyregion/new-york-city-hurricane-evacuation-zones.html.

3. Paul M. Barrett, "It's Global Warming, Stupid," *Bloomberg Businessweek,*
    November 1, 2012, http://www.businessweek.com/articles/2012-11-01
    /its-global-warming-stupid.
4. "Selected Significant Climate Anomalies and Events September 2012,"
    NOAA,   http://www.ncdc.noaa.gov/sotc/service/global/extremes/201209
    .gif.
5. "Why So Wild?" *National Geographic,* http://ngm.nationalgeographic
    .com/2012/09/extreme-weather/data-charts.
6. Peter Miller, "Weather Gone Wild," *National Geographic,* http://ngm
    .nationalgeographic.com/2012/09/extreme-weather/miller-text.
7. "Press Release: North America Most Affected by Increase in Weather-
    related Natural Catastrophes," Munich Re, October 17, 2012, http://www
    .munichre.com/en/media_relations/press_releases/2012/2012_10_17_press
    _release.aspx.
8. Munich Re calculates 2011 total weather disaster losses at nearly $150
    billion.
9. Clifford Kraus, "Exxon and Shell Earnings, Hurt by Natural Gas, Are
    Helped by Refining," *New York Times,* November 1, 2012, http://nytimes
    .com/2012/11/02/business/energy-environment/earnings-at-oil-giants
    -helped-by-refining.html?_r=0; "20 Most Profitable Companies," CNN
    Money,   http://money.cnn.com/galleries/2011/fortune/1104/gallery.fortune
    500_most_profitable.fortune/index.html.
10. "Global Trends 2030: Alternative Worlds," National Intelligence Council,
    http://www.acus.org/files/global-trends-2030-nic-lo.pdf.
11. Elisabeth Rosenthal, "As Biofuel Demand Grows, So Do Guatemala's
    Hunger Pangs," *New York Times,* January 5, 2013, http://www.nytimes
    .com/2013/01/06/science/earth/in-fields-and-markets-guatemalans-feels
    -squeeze-of-biofuel-demand.html?pagewanted=all&_r=0.
12. "HSBC: Is There Enough Water to Fuel China's Power Expansion?"
    China Water Risk, September 19, 2012, http://chinawaterrisk.org/notices
    /china-water-risk-and-hsbc-no-power-no-water-report/.
13. "Water Hungry Coal," Report 2012, Greenpeace, http://www.greenpeace
    .org/africa/Global/africa/publications/coal/WaterHungryCoal.pdf.
14. "Secretary Clinton Calls for Cooperation on Shared Waters," U.S. De-
    partment of State, September 25, 2012, http://www.state.gov/r/pa/prs
    /ps/2012/09/198159.htm.
15. "Water Security: The Water-Energy-Food-Climate Nexus," World Economic
    Forum, http://www.weforum.org/reports/water-security-water-energy-food
    -climate-nexus.

7 THE CUTTING EDGE OF INNOVATION

1. "What Do You Mean by the Term Biomimicry?" Biomimicry Institute,
    http://www.biomimicryinstitute.org/about-us/what-do-you-mean-by-the
    -term-biomimicry.html.
2. Interface, http://www.interfaceflor.asia/about.php.
3. Tom Randall, "How to Clean Five Billion Pounds of Carpeting: Interface,"
    Bloomberg, June 4, 2012, http://www.bloomberg.com/news/2012-06-04
    /how-to-clean-five-billion-pounds-of-carpeting-interface.html.
4. "Photosynthesis: Cooke's koki'o," Ask Nature, May 7, 2012, http://www
    .asknature.org/strategy/ee4e268a5a0fe3861f6d1f5ae21ea608.

5. "Biomimicry:HVACInspiredbyTermites,"Sustainablog,December12,2007, http://sustainablog.org/2007/12/biomimicry-hvac-inspired-by-termites/.
6. Better Place, www.betterplace.com/.
7. "Better Place Focus," Renault, http://www.renault.com/en/groupe/develop pement-durable/environnement/pages/focus-better-place.aspx.
8. "Better Place Takes First Step In China," Better Place, http://www.better place.com/press-room/better-place-takes-first-step-in-china.
9. "Waste and Recycling Facts," Clean Air Council, http://www.cleanair.org /Waste/wasteFacts.html.
10. Ibid.
11. "Recycling and Waste," Environment Nova Scotia, http://www.gov.ns.ca /nse/waste/.
12. Stephen Leahy, "Study: Recycling Cost Overstated," *Wired Magazine,* September 13, 2004, http://www.wired.com/science/discoveries/news/2004/09 /64900?currentPage=all.
13. "Composting," Municipality of Colchester, http://www.colchester.ca /composting.
14. "Fecal Fest: 2012 Fall Fecal Fest," Woodland Park Zoo, www.zoo.org /fecalfest.
15. ZooDoo, http://www.zoodoo.co.nz/index.php.
16. "Water, Sanitation & Hygiene," Bill & Melinda Gates Foundation, http:// www.gatesfoundation.org/watersanitationhygiene/Pages/home.aspx.
17. Steve Yacchino, "Thieves Seek Restaurants' Used Fryer Oil," *New York Times,* January 7, 2012, http://www.nytimes.com/2012/01/08/us/restau rants-used-fryer-oil-attracting-thieves.html.
18. "How 20 Popular Websites Looked When They Launched," *The Telegraph,* September 2, 2009, http://www.telegraph.co.uk/technology/6125914/How -20-popular-websites-looked-when-they-launched.html.
19. Jeanne Clark, "Patent Pools: A Solution to the Problem of Access in Bio-technology Patents?" U.S. Patent and Trademark Office, December 5, 2000, www.uspto.gov/patents/law/patent_pools.pdf.
20. "Apollo 11 Moon Landing: Ten Facts About Armstrong, Aldrin and Col-lins' Mission," *The Telegraph,* July 18, 2009, http://www.telegraph.co.uk /science/space/5852237/Apollo-11-Moon-landing-ten-facts-about-Arm strong-Aldrin-and-Collins-mission.html.
21. Sematech, http://www.sematech.org.
22. "Chip Makers Join DoCoMo in Smartphone Venture," *Wall Street Journal,* December 28, 2011, http://online.wsj.com/article/SB10001424052970203 391104577123481823479756.html.
23. "Draft decision -/CP.15, Proposal by the President, Copenhagen Accord," United Nations Climate Change Conference 2009, http://unfccc.int/re source/docs/2009/cop15/eng/l07.pdf.
24. "SEC Issues Interpretive Guidance on Disclosure Related to Business or Le-gal Developments Regarding Climate Change," U.S. Securities & Exchange Commission, 2010, http://www.sec.gov/news/press/2010/2010-15.htm.

8   WHY DON'T WE?

1. "Natural Resource Conflict," RESOLVE, http://www.resolv.org/our-work /issues/natural-resource-conflict.

INDEX